W9-CDU-012

The Magic of Groundhog Day

The Magic of Groundhog Day

Transform Your World Day By Day

PAUL HANNAM

WATERSIDE PRODUCTIONS

Copyright © TK

ISBN 10: 1-933754-57-5
ISBN 13: 978-1-933754-57-4

Book design by Mark McGarry,
Texas Type & Book Works

Set in Cochin

FIRST EDITION

Dedication

Contents

Foreword   00

Preface   00

Introduction   00

CHAPTER ONE   The Groundhog Day Effect   00

CHAPTER TWO   Living Our Own Groundhog Day   00

CHAPTER THREE   The Magic of Paying Attention   00

CHAPTER FOUR   The Magic of Repetition   00

CHAPTER FIVE   The Magic of Acceptance   00

CHAPTER SIX   The Magic of Creativity   00

CHAPTER SEVEN   The Magic of Love   00

CHAPTER EIGHT   A Magical Life   00

CHAPTER NINE   A Magical Career   00

Conclusion   00

Foreword
by Danny Rubin

It went something like this:

If a person could live forever—and by "forever" I mean a really, really, really long time, and certainly longer than a single lifetime—would that person fundamentally change? How much? In which way? And why?

And who? Which somebody gets to take this eternal journey? Dramatically, he should be somebody with a long way to travel; there should be a good distance from who he is to who he will be. Perhaps he should begin as a jerk Self-centered. An emotional child. And his journey should feel long, like a young man's journey through life.

And when to begin this journey? A thousand years ago? Next Tuesday? Does his life move from the French Revolution through some slice of the present and onward to some future world I would have to make up from scratch? That would be a very sloppy experiment, expensive to film, kind of boring, and a whole lot of work.

Wait a second . . . what if his entire life's journey took place on one single repeating day?

And then my head exploded.

Ever since that moment I have been surrounded by the magic of *Groundhog Day*.

First there was the movie itself. My screenplay had served its purpose as fishing bait in the Hollywood sea, attracting nibbles and finally landing some of the biggest fish in the pond. To my delight, the director was a writing director and he knew how to make a tasty Hollywood meal from my yummy bait. The lead actor is a comic genius, a movie star who was ready for some of the best work of his career. The entire process was filled with dedicated professionals who all seemed to genuinely enjoy the project.

And it all worked, which it doesn't always. Whether it worked because of me or in spite of me we screenwriters never know *Groundhog Day* is undeniably a wonderful movie. Then there were the letters. That was fun. Fan mail. This is typical for movie stars but a little unusual for the screenwriter. I started a file on my computer that I had to call something, so I called it my "Flounder File," as in the Bullwinkle quip: "Fan mail from some flounder?" I didn't mean any disrespect, but I was too embarrassed to put "Fan Mail" on my desktop, and "Groundhog Day Correspondence" was too long.

The first letter I got was from a monk in Germany.

A monk.

In Germany.

The next one was from a young couple who studied the Kabbalah, a practice of Jewish mysticism. Another was from a professor of philosophy in Pennsylvania. Letters began to arrive from psychologists, who prescribed the movie to their patients; from Buddhists, who voted it the best Buddhist movie ever; from Catholics, who were genuinely surprised that I was not a Catholic.

This is just a movie we're talking about, right? The comedy? With Bill Murray?

I compared notes with director Harold Ramis, my occasional guide, big brother, fellow folkie and groundhog wrangler, the maker of The Movie blessed be he. Harold was receiving the same kind of mail. It wasn't exactly surprising; people were getting from the film a lot of what we had intended, and it was most certainly gratifying. But the letters were remarkable. We were being sent serious scholarly works, articles from professional journals, sermons . . . NOT your usual fan mail. I was learning a great deal about what I had intended when I wrote the movie!

What I really learned was that everybody was applying the concepts from *Groundhog Day* to their own lives and disciplines, everyone seeing themselves in the movie and the movie in themselves.

How cool is that?

Then came the phone calls and clippings from friends and family and flounders. Broadcasts and articles from news bureaus and publications all over the world were using the phrase "It's like *Groundhog Day.*" The phrase was being used by diplomats, by academics, and by clergy; in schools and prisons and army units; in sports sections and food sections. After a while, hardly anybody bothered to send me clippings—too much, too many. "It's like *Groundhog Day*" had entered the lexicon.

So, why? Why does the movie work? Why do so many people connect to it, and why does everybody connect to it in his own language?

I would not presume to tell you.

But this little comedy has somehow touched a deep and common chord in people from seemingly different walks of life and modes of thought. My mind wanders: common chord. Common ground . . .

Groundhog.

And here we are, fellow humans, in a world where many of the problems we encounter seem to be familiar, repetitive, and intractable. "Haven't we been here before?" we ask. "Isn't it Groundhog Day again—in politics, in business, in marriage, on Planet Earth?"

If we are stuck—either personally or as a society—then how do we get unstuck? Out of the loop, over the hump? One common effect of the movie is that it makes us feel hopeful and optimistic: if Phil can transform his day, perhaps we can as well. And perhaps we can.

The Magic of Groundhog Day is Paul Hannam's exploration of this Groundhog phenomenon, this resonating experience,

this . . . it's hard to know what to call it. It's unprecedented.
There is an intersection with so many things: philosophy,
psychology, religion, science, literature . . .

That's a lot to handle, but to my pleasure I found Paul
to be perfectly tailored to this task. As a fellow of Oxford
University, businessman, environmentalist, dedicated family guy, and unrepentant movie lover, he has certainly
found his place in authoring this book. And, for all his eru-
dition, the word this tall and delightful Englishman uses to
express the effect of *Groundhog Day* on our lives is simply
"magic."

I hope you enjoy the book as I did, are entertained and
stimulated. Whether you are interested in solving the
world's problems, revisiting issues affecting your own life,
or simply peering at the movie from new angles, I invite
you onward through these pages to spend a bit more time
immersing yourself in the magic that is *Groundhog Day*.

Introduction

⌒

On a freezing February day in a small town in Pennsylvania, a broken weatherman endures the worst day of his life. He wakes at six a.m., smashes his alarm clock on the floor, and drags himself to work. Unshaven and unkempt, he delivers his despondent report to the camera concluding with, "There is no way this winter is ever going to end."

With dead eyes and a resigned voice, he tells his producer, Rita, "I've come to the end of me," and then tries to kill himself over and over again. He electrocutes himself with a toaster in his bath, walks in front of a truck, and throws himself off a building. At the end of his tether, death seems like the only way out of the nightmare he perceives his life to be.

Later, on the exact same freezing February day in the same small town in Pennsylvania, the same man enjoys the best day of his life. He is smartly dressed, and with a happy disposition he delivers his heartfelt report to the camera, this time concluding with, "I couldn't imagine a better fate than a long and lustrous winter."

After his report, he proceeds to spend the day performing acts of kindness. He catches a boy from a falling tree, changes a tire for some old ladies, and saves an important local official from choking.

That evening at a town party, he entertains the crowds with his piano playing and is praised by the same people he used to despise. Rita meets him and says, "You seem to be the most popular person in town." After she has paid top dollar for him at the auction, he sculpts her face in ice and tells her, "No matter what happens tomorrow or for the rest of my life I'm happy now, because I love you."

The man is Phil Connors, the town is Punxsutawney, and the movie is *Groundhog Day*. The town has not changed. The events and the people have not changed. Not even time has changed. The same people perform the same activities and speak the same words. The days are identical except for one thing. Phil has changed.

He has gone from the worst day of his life to the best day of his life, not by changing his outer world, but by changing his inner life. This is the most important lesson of my life, and the movie *Groundhog Day* is the ultimate class in how to live and work.

You too can change a miserable day into a wonderful day. I have written *The Magic of Groundhog Day* to show how you can follow Phil's lead to achieve this transformation in your own life. Like Phil, we can all wake up and discover joy rather than boredom, hope rather than emptiness, and love rather than self-absorption.

The Movie

In *Groundhog Day*, weatherman Phil Connors visits Punxsutawney on February 2 with his TV crew. He is there to cover the annual Groundhog Day ritual and is due to leave right after the event. To his dismay, he cannot leave, trapped by a supernatural force that makes him relive the same day hundreds, maybe thousands, of times. He is caught in the time loop of an endlessly repeating day.

Moreover, Phil is the only person in Punxsutawney who is aware of his imprisonment in time. The rest of the movie shows how he deals with his predicament—and the extraordinary change he experiences as he repeats the same day again and again.

The movie is growing in popularity every year, in the way that *It's a Wonderful Life* 1946 has become a perennial classic. *Groundhog Day* has developed a similar fan base. Indeed, I can think of no other movie that gets better with more viewings. It is regularly repeated on TV, and DVD sales are still high.

The Profound Meaning of *Groundhog Day*

The story of *Groundhog Day* has many layers, meanings, and interpretations. Like all great stories, it helps us to bet-

ter understand ourselves by describing the human condition in an original and insightful manner. It is so much
deeper than any other comedy or love story I know. The
movie is an original interpretation of the timeless story of
rebirth and redemption, made unique by its humor, charm,
and contemporary setting. In an inspiring and highly
entertaining way, it deals with the great questions of our
lives. How do I discover meaning? How do I overcome
fear? How do I find love? How do I change?

As I watched Phil's development, I imagined how I
would respond in the same situation. Indeed, the idea of
confronting endless recurrence intrigued and fascinated
me in a way that I could not fully understand at first. It was
several years and many more viewings before I realized
that this was much more than a romantic comedy. The
movie went beyond a Capraesque salute to small-town
America. It offered even more than a tale of personal
change and the overcoming of psychological obstacles.
Phil's literal imprisonment in a recurring day is a powerful
symbol for a condition that affects millions. The way in
which he breaks free of his imprisonment also reveals timeless and universal principles for how we might progress, as
individuals and organizations—and by extension—societies.

Furthermore, discussions with Danny Rubin, the co-
screenwriter of *Groundhog Day*, deepened my understanding of the movie's themes. This book has emerged from
those talks, in addition to my notes and the change and

leadership courses I have taught at the University of Oxford. Groundhog Day itself is an annual ritual that takes place toward the end of winter in the days when cabin fever can take the joy out of our lives. It is a time when we can either fixate on a dark, cold future or look forward to bright days ahead. The groundhog is a predictor of six more weeks of winter or an early spring. Of course, it cannot really control the weather, but tradition holds that if it fails to see its shadow, we will be able to break out of our humdrum routine. If it does see its shadow, we will remain stuck. This reinforces the idea that our fate is out of our hands, that external forces will dictate what is going to happen to us.

Spending more time indoors in winter, we have more time to think. Do we focus on the positive or negative? Are we suffering from cabin fever, or are we actively planning and looking forward to the next stage of our lives?

The Groundhog Day Effect

All of us are living in our own version of *Groundhog Day* to some extent. I call this the Groundhog Day Effect, a phenomenon that affects individuals, groups, organizations, and human civilization itself. For many, this is the daily grind of endlessly repetitive tasks, mind-numbing encounters with the same people, and meaningless activities and conversations. This effect keeps us feeling stuck and powerless to change. By recognizing and understanding how our repetitive patterns of thought and action produce those negative feelings, we understand why change is so difficult.

Not long before I started writing this book, I experienced an unsettling revelation about the power of the effect. For the first time, I read the entire contents of a diary I had kept for six years. I read about all the places I had been—from Sydney and Singapore to San Francisco and Santa Fe. I read about the hundreds of people I had met through my work in business, training, and university.

During that time, both my dad and my father-in-law had died. My mother-in-law had suffered a major stroke and my mother had moved to a retirement community. My daughter and son had grown from children to eighteen and sixteen years old respectively. My wife and I had both turned forty. We had lost two dogs and gained another. We had moved our home and arranged immigration to the United States. I had written my first book. It appeared that a great deal had happened and changed in my life—or had it?

I noticed something else in the diaries. In between the details of my activities, I had written more personal observations. As I examined them, I realized to my dismay that, whereas much had changed in my outer life, almost nothing had changed in my inner life.

In February of year six, I was still writing about the same concerns as February of year one! I still had the same hopes, fears, and regrets. How could I be happy? How could I deal with middle age? Why was I feeling so tired? What would happen to my children? My diary entries followed cyclical patterns of oscillation between happiness and sadness, optimism and pessimism, action and withdrawal. In my inner life, I was trapped in my own version of Phil Connors' Groundhog Day.

Then I noticed that the patterns remained, irrespective of where I was or what I was doing. Being in Hawaii did not break me free, nor did seeing my first book in print. Underneath the superficial variety of my life was an inescapable sameness. As the French expression puts it: *Plus ça change, plus c'est la même chose.* The more things change, the more they stay the same.

As I considered my predicament, I thought again about *Groundhog Day*. The movie no longer felt like just the story of Phil Connors. It felt like the story of my life. My thinking was repetitive, and in my mind I was essentially reliving the same day over and over again.

Each morning I would wake up feeling that I had little or no control over my moods or actions. I would get up to shower, have breakfast, and then sit down at the computer. The rest of the day would follow the same routine of answering email, surfing the Net, performing administrative tasks, and taking the odd break. Then it was evening, and another day had disappeared. It felt like a trance, as though I was living life unconsciously and missing the whole point of it.

This routine was also very seductive, almost addictive. I did not need to think too much; simply go through the motions. Sometimes I would think that I had to break out of this and make a change, but then I was pulled back into the old patterns that seemed so much stronger than any resolve to change.

The Groundhog Day Effect is largely caused by our unique set of behavioral and thought patterns, which create our personal reality. We do not directly experience the world around us; we experience a personal reality through our senses. Personal reality is a reflection of reality, not reality itself. So, in effect, there are two realities. The reality of what is, the real world, and the world as we see it, our personal reality. We might not repeat the exact day over and over again in our outer lives, yet our personal reality can effectively create the same day again and again in our inner lives.

Once we understand the influence of our personal reality, we can start to break free of the Groundhog Day Effect and experience the magic of *Groundhog Day* instead. When I watch the movie I feel as though I have awakened, and I see a world full of hope, possibilities, and joy. Indeed, we can all let a magical movie bring magic into our lives. *Groundhog Day* offers us the possibility of new realities, and the true magic is that we can change our personal reality.

For twenty-five years I have researched, taught, and practiced personal and organizational change as an academic, consultant, and entrepreneur. I have always wanted to know the answer to two questions: Why do we find it so hard to change? And how we can most effectively change?

The best answers I have found are not in complex theories or obscure journals. No, they are found in the movie *Groundhog Day*. For over a decade, I have used the movie's message to inspire hundreds of people, and I have discussed the academic implications with my students at Oxford University in courses about change and leadership.

I have helped people stuck in the Groundhog Day Effect escape the cycles that keep them trapped. Utilizing the ideas and tools in this book, I have coached people to stop limiting patterns that have kept them in dysfunctional behaviors, relationships, and careers. Moreover, I have helped organizations to break free from damaging cycles of performance and develop "organizational realities" for dealing with employees.

After researching the multiple psychological, philosophical, and organizational dimensions of this wonderful movie, I keep returning to *Groundhog Day* as the best story I know for describing and explaining the process of change. It offers us an extraordinary philosophy to direct us through our lives and careers.

Applying Phil's Transformation to Your Own Life

Groundhog Day is a magical story—not only in the sense of fantastic occurrences such as one day repeating itself endlessly—but in the concepts it can teach as a tale of transformation. This does not mean that Phil Connors was looking to change his life. At the start, he is not ready for change and does not believe he has any problems. He does not have a plan, and reacts to his predicament by trial and error.

Phil changes the way most of us change: in a haphazard, inconsistent, and unplanned manner. This is what makes him such a captivating figure. He is the kind of guy we all know and many of us have been like at some time — a complex person who personifies the best and the worst in us. He is great fun and egotistical. He is romantic and vulgar. He is charming and exasperating, kind and selfish.

Phil represents the contradictions at the heart of human nature. When he uses his foresight of events in Punxsutawney to have fun, seduce women, and manipulate people, we share the fun while berating him for his callousness and arrogance. Through Phil we can explore what it would be like to have supernatural powers and indulge in the fantasy of knowing the future.

Phil can act out our dreams of control, power, and greed. He knows that he can do what he wants and that he will do no real harm to others, as everyone and everything will be the same the next day. He plays out the full spectrum of behaviors in his intense experience, and in doing so reveals deep truths about our lives.

Through his development we can also realize what is most important to us and what we really want — and do not want. As Phil exhausts every comical and clever trick he can conjure up, he starts to run out of steam. He discovers that exclusively seeking his own pleasure eventually brings diminishing returns, and that what he imagines will make him happy rarely does.

Of course, you do not need to go through the same process as Phil. You can choose your responses. Yet the beauty of the movie is that Phil chooses the responses that most of us would. He is no saint or hero with great spiritual wisdom. He is an ordinary man searching to make the best of what at first seems like a very bad deal.

In the end, the day does not change, the location does not change, and the townspeople do not change. It is Phil who changes. His magical journey involves no travel, only a change in his mind and heart. He turns the worst day into the best day of his life, simply by thinking and acting differently.

This is the real magic of *Groundhog Day*. Indeed, film is the perfect medium for this lesson. For we have always sought magic in movies. During the Great Depression of the 1930s, millions went to the movies to escape from their dreary lives. For a few hours, they could forget about unemployment and poverty. They were transported to amazing locations, entranced by beautiful actors, and entertained by exciting adventures. The problem was that the magic would wear off quickly once they left the theater.

It seems that *Groundhog Day* is based on an impossible, supernatural premise: time stops and we are caught in an eternally repeating day. The real, practical magic is how Phil handles the time loop, and how, at long last, he changes. The phenomenon of the time loop is simply the trigger for the magical change within Phil.

The good news is that we can transport the magic of *Groundhog Day* into our own lives. We have the conditions, resources, and tools to re-create the transformation that Phil goes through. We have the same power as Phil. We do not need the *Groundhog Day* time loop to jumpstart this process; what we need is Phil's awakening and transformation.

The real voyage of discovery consists not in seeking new landscapes, but in having new eyes.

MARCEL PROUST

The magic is there for us all the time. Life is enchanting and miraculous if we simply tune in to it. The magic of *Groundhog Day* is the everyday magic that surrounds us all. Each day contains the seeds of magic.

You can choose to experience the magic, or ignore it. How do you want to live today, then tomorrow and the next day? Even if you do not know the quantity of days left in the rest of your life, you will now be able to improve the quality of those days by discovering the magic in each one.

We can learn this, and a lot more quickly than Phil does. We can re-create Phil's joy on February 3 by using the everyday magic at our disposal. Every day is already magical, whether we choose to experience it or not. This does not mean that we will feel enchanted every day, simply that we will have the skills to get out of a rut and better appreciate the magic that is already present.

Phil learns how to pay attention to the magic around him. To use repetition to his advantage. To accept what he can and cannot change. To discover and express his creativity. And to find authentic meaning and love. In so doing, he creates his own magical life with the same resources he had used to create misery and despair. This is magic we can all practice. What follows is my guide to help us break free of the Groundhog Day Effect and live the life we choose to live, not the life we were conditioned to live.

The Magic of Groundhog Day

CHAPTER ONE

The Groundhog Day Effect

"Well, what if there was no tomorrow? There wasn't one today."

When he becomes aware that he is stuck in a time loop, Phil visits a bowling alley and starts talking with two local drunks. He complains about his fate. "How would you feel," he asks his pals, "if you woke up every morning and it was the same awful day and nothing you ever did made the slightest difference because nothing meant anything?" One of the drunks sadly replies, "That about sums it up for me."

Does this sum it up for you? Do you feel that whatever you do makes little difference and that nothing means anything? Do you feel trapped or stagnant? Do you seem to be living the same day over and over again? Do you believe that life could be much better?

Phil's life is repetitive and, truth be told, most of us face the same predicament. While we might not be stuck in a time loop, we may be more entrenched in self-limiting patterns than we would like to admit. We believe that we are autonomous, independent individuals in charge of our lives, and don't like to consider that our actions could be determined by anything other than our free will. I have named this predicament the Groundhog Day Effect, and I believe it is a characteristic of the human condition. It seems to describe and even explain many of the chronic problems people face, such as anxiety, stress, dissatisfaction, lack of meaning, and loneliness. How many people feel trapped in an unrelenting cycle of commuting, working, paying the bills, collapsing in front of the TV, and sleeping?

In many years of working as a consultant to a variety of organizations, I had witnessed this firsthand, even if I had not yet named it. Hundreds of people I met felt trapped in routine jobs. And they were working for companies trapped in outdated strategies and management thinking. Concerned exclusively with short-term growth, they had grown complacent and stagnant in ever-narrowing circles.

Many executives are stuck in their professional and personal lives. I know the vice president of Sales at a successful technology business who leaves home at six a.m. and returns at ten p.m. five days a week. Every day he wakes up with the luxury of freedom, yet spends the day following a set routine like an automaton. He gets up at the same time, commutes at the same time, surrendering to the demands of traffic and his business. His days are structured by repetitive activities, each minute scheduled, often months in advance. Shuffling from one meeting to another and battling against a never-ending barrage of emails, calls, and deadlines, he has exchanged his freedom for the golden handcuffs of corporate imprisonment.

On the weekend he works similar hours, and when he is with his family he is permanently on his cell phone. He is one of the thousands of money-rich, time-poor executives stuck in various loops since birth. He has followed a predetermined trajectory from school through college to the boardroom.

He has habituated to a lifestyle that is potentially life threatening. He is always restless, running around in circles, and on edge. He has adapted to this dysfunctional, unsatisfying and harmful lifestyle and cannot imagine living any other way. When challenged, people such as this executive always explain and justify their behavior by saying that they will "change soon" or that they are only doing it until "the big deal comes in." The dilemma is that they rarely if ever change; they continue to delude themselves into believing that everything will turn out fine in the end.

My friend is stuck in a never-ending loop, locked in to complex socioeconomic and cultural systems that shape every aspect of his life. Normally, he is unaware of these patterns, because he is so immersed in activity that his routine has taken charge of his life. Other times, he knows he is trapped and when relaxing over a beer he talks about breaking free. The problem is that he cannot. The repetitive cycles are just too strong, and the Groundhog Day Effect too insidious. Unfortunately, just being aware of his predicament does not lead to release.

My friend, like all of us, is caught in repetitive economic systems that depend on efficiency, control, and predictability. Most of us have to work to earn a living, while many employees feel trapped in routine jobs. This can be demoralizing and lead to chronic stress and illness. I have met employees earning minimum wage holding down three jobs just to put food on the table. Their work is joyless and mind-numbing, with little opportunity for creativity.

Most of us might not bear such direct pressures, yet we pressure ourselves instead, succumbing to the influence of powerful media forces, corporations, and advertising. Every day we are exposed to thousands of commercial messages that influence our self-image, values, and aspirations. We live in a consumer society, and we are judged by how well we do by its rules and norms. We are working longer hours, and commuting farther, to make more money to consume more things that we do not need and—crucially—that are not making us happier. We are better off, yet more unhappy than ever before.[1]

We delude ourselves that our status depends on how much we can consume and how many activities we can cram into a day. Soon we become habituated to the never-ending scramble from one activity to another, to multitasking, and to the constant assault on our senses from emails, messaging, cell phones, and the steady background noise. It might feel normal. It is not magical.

We are also locked in to technological systems that we take for granted. Imagine life without water on tap or electricity at the flick of a switch. Imagine life without your PC, Blackberry, cell phone, or TV. Our technology creates powerful patterns of behavior that dominate our lives, such as Web surfing, sending emails, and driving. Much of our language, fashion, and mind-set is conditioned by technology and the media.

Freedom is what you do with what's been done to you.

JEAN-PAUL SARTRE

Ironically, we are more connected than ever before at a technological level while, at the same time, more disconnected from each other and from ourselves. We are afraid of being alone. We are anxious to not waste time, afraid of stopping our frenetic activity. Above all, we are fearful of confronting ourselves and the deeper questions of our existence beyond the superficial roles we adopt.

This is the case with Phil when he arrives in Punxsutawney. He is caught up in his role as a TV weatherman and disconnected from the real world. Are you so very different? Are you restless? Do you get bored easily? Do you feel guilty if you have nothing to do? Do you find it hard to relax?

Our supposed "independence" is deceptive. In reality, we are dependent on the many systems that form our lives. Unless we are fully aware, we naturally gravitate toward repetitive patterns, encouraged and reinforced by the demands and influences of everyday life. Most of the time, we are not even aware that we are caught up in a cycle. When the truth hits us, we find that getting out is difficult or impossible. In the West we spend billions of dollars simply trying to break free of unwanted habits. Our homes are full of discarded exercise machines and diet books. Bad habits are very hard to break.

The more I spoke to friends and colleagues, the clearer it became that we are all living through our very own *Groundhog Day* to some extent, and that repetition and feeling trapped are part of the human experience. Sometimes this effect is obvious. There are many millions of people who are literally trapped in repetitive patterns of living by external forces such as imprisonment, slavery, serious illness, or poverty. Every day they wake up to the same, unending struggle for survival.

In the "land of the free" how free are you? How much of what you do each day is voluntary, and how much is involuntary? How many of your activities do you choose to do, and how many are determined by the demands of others? Is your life dominated by duty and responsibility? How much choice do you have, or think you have?

Life Is Repetitive

At the most basic level of existence, humans are compromised by the need for repetition. Our bodies depend on repetitive respiratory, circulatory, and digestive systems among many others. Every day we need to eat, drink, and sleep to survive. Every few seconds we need to breathe.

We are also part of a larger repetitive system. The earth itself is in a loop going round the sun. Night follows day, and our survival depends on natural cycles such as reproduction and photosynthesis. The majority of the world's population depends on regular weather patterns, particularly predictable rainfall.

Despite our diversity of race, culture, and history, repetitive behaviors are an attribute of human nature itself. Evolutionary psychologists believe that we all share universal traits such as fear, anger, and disgust, and that our behavior is far more repetitive and biologically determined than we care to believe. They argue that we are all hardwired to display strong preferences for status, power, beauty, and security.

At home and at work, these preferences motivate much of what we do. Science and technology might have led to great progress, yet human nature has not changed for thousands of years. We are still caught in the same struggles to overcome our fears and to find meaning.

Outer and Inner Repetition

A repetitive pattern in and of itself is not necessarily harmful. Civilization would collapse without the repetitive patterns necessary to the supply of food and energy. As an individual, a regular structure is fine if you are happy in your routine. The difficulty arises if you are not happy, if you are not at peace, if you see no magic in everyday life. It is not so much outer repetition but inner repetition—repetitive thought patterns—that create the Groundhog Day Effect.

When we are oblivious to the magic of everyday life, caught in destructive and repetitive thought patterns, our first tendency is often to blame our predicament on our jobs, where we live, or on our partners. We believe that by changing our external circumstances we will break free from the loop.

Sometimes circumstances or other people are to blame. We change jobs, relocate, or separate from our partner. This might fix the problem, yet more frequently it only leads to a temporary improvement. Soon after, we are liable to revert to the same old habits and routine. Although it may be satisfying to blame others, superficial repetitive patterns are rarely the cause of the problem. No, the problem tends to lie at a deeper level, in patterns that may have existed our entire lives.

Ever notice how when you visit your parents or siblings you tend to slip back into childlike patterns of behavior? You might also have been married multiple times but sadly discovered that the same interpersonal dynamics, the same arguments, and the same frustrations consistently resurfaced. Or you might drift from one job to another and fail to perform successfully for similar reasons.

For many years, I would start a new job or create a new

business as a way of fixing my life. For the first few weeks or months everything was exciting, and the buzz gave me a huge rush of adrenaline. By constantly moving, I could avoid dealing with the deeper patterns. Inevitably this led to tremendous stress, then illness, and I would crash soon after. I would take a few weeks to recover. Everything would be calm and balanced for a while, and then I would be off again on another pursuit of the Big Answer to my life.

It has taken me many years to recognize the deeper patterns of the Groundhog Day Effect. I realized that I was caught in short-term rep-etitions such as addiction to new ideas and a compulsion to respond to emails immediately. I was also caught in much deeper longer-term patterns such as the constant search for a new project to make me happy.

> *Insanity: doing the same thing over and over again and expecting different results.*
>
> —ALBERT EINSTEIN

The beauty of *Groundhog Day* is that Phil is literally trapped; he is forced to become self-aware of his beliefs and behavior. Since nothing changes in the outer world, he can see his inner patterns more clearly. Our challenge is to rec-ognize these patterns in a world where there might be a lot of outer change, yet our inner lives much remain the same.

The Symptoms of Groundhog Day Effect

If you ever feel like you are stuck in a rut or just sleepwalk-ing through life, you could be suffering from the psychological and physical stresses resulting from Groundhog Day Effect. Ever have the feeling of being stuck, going through the motions, and being controlled by habits?

Ever have the feeling of reliving the same day even if the place, people, and events are different? This is the difference between external time and your inner time. External time might be moving forward while you feel stuck in your own independent chronology. The content of your day changes while your thoughts and emotions stay the same. You are experiencing in your inner life what Phil experiences in the movie.

After many years of reflecting on this phenomenon, I have identified the following three symptoms of Groundhog Day Effect. Maybe you recognize one or more in your own life?

1. The Sense That Your Thoughts Are Compulsive

In *Groundhog Day*, Phil makes lots of changes and tries many activities, yet his thought patterns and emotions remain the same until near the end. His mind is consumed with one compulsive, overriding thought: "What's in it for me?" He might be thinking about the potential bank robbery one day, getting drunk the following day, or seducing Rita the next day. The content might change, yet the patterns of thinking do not.

I know an older lady in her seventies who travels all the time, yet her inner life is static. Her thoughts are the same as yesterday and the day before. She is preoccupied with endless, repetitive self-talk. She believes her life is unfair and wishes her past could have been different. The constant trips are temporary diversions from her emotional pain.

Her inner life is repetitive. She visits many countries, yet spends her time living in her head. In effect, her inner days resemble the events in *Groundhog Day*. Her habitual thoughts, attitudes, and actions create the landscape of her everyday experience. She has created her own story and relives her childhood, blaming her parents and her ex-husband for what went wrong. Unless she replaces this story and changes her habits, she can never escape the Groundhog Day Effect, no matter how far she travels or how many new people she meets.

2. A Sense of Living on Automatic Pilot

Phil is living on automatic pilot when he arrives in Punxsutawney. He is not conscious of the town, the people, or the festival. He is just going through the motions of his job to get out as quickly as possible.

I know a friend who seems to be on automatic pilot too, living his days in a trance. He does not seem conscious of what is going on around him and rushes headfirst into conditioned responses and activities. When I speak to him he does not listen; his mind is elsewhere and his eyes dart left to right. Marooned in his office, he spends his days lost in thoughts, hopes, fears, anxieties, and plans, oblivious to the passage of time

Maybe he believes he can accomplish more by not thinking about what he is doing. The disadvantage is that he is not engaged in the moment-by-moment unfolding of his life. He uses the mental space that his routines provide to get stuck in frequently negative patterns of thought. He gets up each morning and, instead of being on the lookout for the groundhog that may signal spring is coming, he focuses on all the things in his life that indicate there will be six more weeks, months, even years of winter. Even on a summer's day he is weighed down by the bleak, cold, and dark winter's day he brings with him.

Like my friend, we are all on automatic pilot to a large extent. We regularly complete tasks without thinking and converse without listening. When we perform a simple action like taking a shower, we are on automatic pilot. We follow the same routine of washing and then drying ourselves. We start with the left arm first, then the right arm, then the torso, then the left leg, and so on.

When we are like this all the time, we avoid deeper questions about our lives. The constant buzz, rush, and multitasking mask our authentic feelings. The "activity trap" restricts our experience to a narrow spectrum of thoughts and emotions. We might reduce our anxieties and fears by staying constantly busy and distracted, but we pay a great price. We settle for a familiar, comfortable routine that numbs the pain. The downside is that it also numbs our joy and passion, taking the magic from our lives.

Unintentionally, we create our own *Groundhog Day*; we surrender our freedom in return for protection from pain and fear. Indeed, this universal dilemma has been recognized by modern social commentators, and also by various spiritual traditions. The Buddhist concept of *Samsara* means to wander around in circles; it is our fate until we learn to awaken. George Gurdjieff, the famous mystic, used the term "waking-sleep" to refer to our lack of awareness, believing that this was the normal, lower state of human beings.

P. D. Ouspensky, who interpreted Gurdjieff's teachings wrote: "All the absurdities and all the contradictions of people, and of human life in general, become explained when we realize that people live in sleep, do everything in sleep, and do not know that they are asleep."[2]

3. A Sense of Being Stuck

Phil is stuck in the town of Punxsutawney and cannot escape. He is faced with real, fixed boundaries of time and place. We all get stuck; sometimes we are aware of it and sometimes we are oblivious to it. At work we get stuck in limiting habits like avoiding risk; at home we get stuck in damaging patterns like having the same weekly argument with our partner about the household budget. Most of us can name friends or acquaintances who have been stuck in unhappy marriages and jobs for years, paralyzed by the burdens of guilt and obligation.

A former colleague of mine was stuck in her career. She had lost all hope, seeing no way out of a job she loathed and an organization that exploited her vulnerabilities. She felt powerless to change, and as she got older she found it harder to get out of her rut. Having settled for a comfort zone of familiar habits, she was suffering from what is often called a midlife crisis.

> *Most men lead lives of quiet desperation and go to the grave with the song still in them.*
>
> HENRY DAVID THOREAU

It is certainly possible to interpret Phil Connors' predicament in this way. He is a man in his forties who does not seem at ease with himself. He is facing what psychologist Erik Erikson described as "stagnation," which leads people to become self-obsessed and to feel alienated and trapped.

We can unintentionally become trapped by our own imaginary boundaries, which include our beliefs, thoughts, and behaviors. We build our own prisons to protect ourselves from dealing with our fears and anxieties. When we are stuck it feels like we are bogged down and cannot move forward. We feel weighed down by duties and responsibilities, constricted to a narrow range of experiences and choices. It feels like neither we nor time are moving forward. We are just getting through the day.

When we are stuck we become set in our ways. Habitual thinking, feeling, and behaviors also set us in time like Phil.

At the time we developed these habits, usually in childhood, we became set in the time. And over the years, our early conditioning may have led to rigid opinions and closed-mindedness. We wonder if we are living our chosen lives or lives determined by our parents, schools, and culture.

We are also at the mercy of forces beyond our control such as accidents, illness, and random events. The issue is how we respond to this uncertainty. Do we feel like victims of circumstance, or do we feel like we have some control?

Power and Happiness

Sometimes powerlessness can be liberating in subtle ways. Phil is forced to accept that he has no control over time and place, and this leads him to focus more on what he can control. Forced repetition might reduce choice, but it can also reduce confusion and lead to insight into what is really important.

A sense of powerlessness affects us in subtle ways. We become imprisoned by our duties. We "have to" be in Denver for the conference next week although we believe it to be pointless. We "must" accept our neighbors' invitation for dinner even though we don't like them. And we are "forced" to stay in the job we hate to pay off the mortgage on our new vacation home. When we think and talk in this way we become prisoners of our own limiting rules, and even our language. We think and act as though we are no longer in charge of our minds or our lives.

Sometimes the flow of thoughts is so strong and so constant that it prevents us from being effective in any area of life. Phil symbolizes our struggle to break free of our conditioning. The good news is that just as Phil Connors broke free of the endlessly repeating February 2 in *Groundhog Day*, you too can break free of the repetitive patterns in your life that have locked you into compulsive thinking, living on autopilot, and feeling stuck. All you need is to rediscover the magic in your life.

CHAPTER TWO

Living Our Own Groundhog Day

When Phil arrives in Punxsutawney, he thinks of the town as dull and full of "hicks," while Rita sees it as charming and fun. The town is the same; only their perceptions are different. Like many of us, Phil has developed a perspective of the world that denies him happiness and fulfillment. In the words of the drunk at the bar, he is a "glass-is-half-empty kind of guy."

At first Phil sees the downside of everything. He is stuck in a place he despises with people he has nothing but contempt for. Everyone else is having a great time, enjoying the festival. So why is Phil so unhappy? It is not being stuck in Punxsutawney that makes him unhappy—it is being stuck in his habitual thinking.

Personal Reality Determines Your Quality of Life

Spending Groundhog Day in Punxsutawney is not part of his career plan. This is a man who is seen by his colleagues as a "prima donna." His self-importance is so great that he claims at one point, "I make the weather!" On this occasion, he is obviously not in control of the weather, since he is unable to leave town due to a blizzard. So now he is not just "wasting" one day but will be forced to stay for a second night in Punxsutawney, feeling frustrated and angry.

Phil's belief that he is in charge is in conflict with the reality of his life: he cannot leave town. His inner life and outer lives are at odds. He is stuck literally and metaphorically. He has shut himself off from new experiences because he is not experiencing life directly, but through his personal reality, which is driven by his ego. There is little magic in his life. He does not pay attention to the world around him, only to his own needs. He is disinterested in other people unless they can help him get what he wants. Rita summarizes his personality with Sir Walter Scott's withering words in *The Lay of the Last Minstrel*:

> *The wretch, concentred all in self,*
> *Living, shall forfeit fair renown,*
> *And, doubly dying, shall go down*
> *To the vile dust from whence he sprung,*
> *Unwept, unhonour'd and unsung.*

The movie is the story of how Phil escapes from the Groundhog Day Effect and discovers the magic of

Groundhog Day instead. Phil escapes the Groundhog Day time loop by transforming himself, and he does this by transforming his personal reality.

From Perception to Reality

The Groundhog Day Effect is the product of our unique system of perceptions, thoughts, attitudes, emotions, memories, knowledge, and values. This system forms our *personal reality*. Like all of us, Phil does not directly experience the world around him; he experiences a personal reality through his senses. His personal reality is a powerful filter system where his perception is filtered through experience, attitudes, thoughts, and focus of attention It is a reflection of reality, not reality itself. So, in effect, there are two realities. The reality of what is, the real world, and the world as we see it, our personal reality. We build our personal reality to make sense of the real world, and see reality reflected in it.

How we feel about ourselves and about today depends on our personal reality. Since our reality operates at an unconscious level, it is unlikely that we are aware of the forces that drive our daily behavior. Our realities are responsible for the characteristics of the Groundhog Day Effect. They create patterns of repetitive behaviors and thoughts; they create the feeling of living on automatic pilot because we have disconnected from reality and plugged into our own version of it.

When we are stuck in our internal reality, this creates our external one too. Therefore, it can feel as if we are powerless when, in fact, we are not. It can feel as if we are stuck when, in fact, we are not. It can feel as if things are hopeless when, in fact, they are anything but. When we experience the Groundhog Day Effect, our personal reality is in charge. We may even feel as if we have been taken over by someone or something else.

The Roots of Personal Reality

As children, we create our reality in order to protect ourselves and cope with life. As we mature into adulthood, this reality is of less value, yet we still tend to cling to familiar patterns and their expected outcomes. We crave security, approval, and love. Yet often we are denied these, and we learn to shut down our emotions to avoid a repetition of the pain. Over the years, this is reinforced by the defensive patterns of our unconscious mind. The problem is that what works for a child rarely works for an adult.

I once worked with someone who never took risks and never sought a promotion because he had been mocked at school for trying to stand out. Once hurt, he had spent his life trying to avoid pain by staying in his comfort zone. The same coping mechanism that had protected him as a child, now held him back as an adult. He stayed safe to an extent, but lost out on personal growth and satisfying relationships. He was trapped by his narrow, self-centered perspectives, unable to experience genuine emotion or empathy for others.

As part of our evolution, we learned simple rules to survive. We deliberately narrowed our choices to deal with threats so we would not waste valuable time analyzing those choices. The classic example of this is the fight-or-flight response. When humans are faced with a challenge, our first reaction is normally to fight or to flee. This instinctual mechanism, which we share it with other species, has helped us to survive for hundreds of thousands of years.

We all know people who are "fighters." Their reality seems to reinforce the need for conflict, and they tend to be dominant, competitive, and status-seeking individuals. I know many businesspeople who are only happy if they are winning. Life is a game in which they have to be the victor. They often mistake normal everyday problems for threats to their survival, as their brains cannot distinguish between a minor dispute and life-or-death danger.

When they become managers they often stay stuck in their competitive, win-lose mentality. Since they believe their success is dependent on other people failing, they constantly judge and criticize others. Because they cannot bear their own people to outshine them, they undermine their team's morale, which leads to poor performance and problems with staff retention.

At the opposite end of the scale are those whose natural instinct is flight. They always back down, avoiding confrontation and conflict at all cost. In contrast to fighters, "fleers" confuse simple disagreements with threats to their survival. Their overriding need for security keeps them trapped in uncomfortable situations and relationships.

Over the years, they create a reality that continually scans a hostile world for potential dangers, paralyzing them with fear and apprehension.

Moreover, I have often seen this in organizations where I have worked with managers who cannot confront reality. They hide in their offices, buried in their strategic plans while their customers desert them and their market share collapses. They hope the market will pick up, and when it doesn't it is often too late to make the necessary changes.

The Importance of Our Personal Reality

Not only do we all have filtering systems that create our reality, everyone has a different system. For example, I remember watching *Groundhog Day* with a friend who thought it was a mildly amusing Bill Murray comedy. What I found extraordinary, especially the repetition, he found uninteresting. When I laughed out loud during the scene when Phil meets Ned Ryerson, my friend was silent.

We were both watching the film, but through the different filters of our personal realties. We both saw the same visuals and heard the same dialogue. But we had different expectations and standards for evaluating the movie, and consequently different interpretations and opinions once we had seen it.

We use your memories, attitudes, values, and other preferences to make sense of our experience. At the perceptual level, we cannot take in every sensory experience without facing overload. So, we have to select what we are seeing, hearing, and feeling. And everyone does this differently. Extend this phenomenon from a movie that only lasts 101 minutes to a lifetime of accumulated experiences, and you will begin to recognize the extraordinary significance of our personal reality.

Your reality determines the quality of our experience. Your thoughts, emotions, and actions work together to build a powerful filter that decides what is good or bad, enjoyable or unpleasant. Over time, this leads to repetitive patterns of automatic thinking, which result in the feeling that you have no control over your life.

Your reality creates its own needs, which you confuse with your genuine needs. If your reality is based on seeking attention, you will always crave attention and approval. With such a relentless need you feel dissatisfied and incomplete, however much attention you get.

Your reality also creates its own boundaries. It structures what you see, hear, and feel. If you seek approval, you will use all your senses to check if people like you or not. Your behavior aims to project favorable impressions, to sell yourself like a commodity, rather than establish genuine, quality relationships.

Your reality also sets its own rules, which can be irrational and lead to ongoing feelings of frustration and dissatisfaction. For example, I have met people who say they will only be happy if they marry a supermodel, and others who will only consider themselves successful if they become a billionaire.

Their reality produces unrealistic expectations and

desires. In effect, their world and the real world are in conflict. It is easier for them to believe the childlike illusion
that the real world should conform to their personal reality, than to accept that their filters were wrong and they
themselves must change. They doom themselves to never-
ending disappointment because, as we learn as adults, it is
impossible for people and events to always turn out the
way we want.

Phil Connors learns this lesson when he loses all power
over the real world, when time stops and he is trapped in
the same day. He tries to get the town to conform to his
plans and desires by manipulating people with his power
and knowledge. He seduces women and robs banks. Yet
these are trivial diversions; he s compelled to face his own
helplessness.

Our reality also limits our experience as it keep us
locked in repetitive patterns that prevent growth and
progress. Each day we are caught in our stories, like passive and predictable characters. If we take a closer look,
we will find that our stories explain why we are unhappy
or not getting what we want. After all, we are the authors
of our reality. In this way, we remain effectively trapped in
the past, further strengthening the Groundhog Day Effect.

Change Is Hard

Our stories make it difficult for us to break free from the
Groundhog Day Effect. At various times of our lives we

might decide that we would like to change. We might want to become more relaxed or more assertive, or we might want to change career or lose weight. So we buy a book or a program, and attend different types of classes.

At first we achieve some success, but our personal reality has its own field of gravity. It will only let us go so far and then pull us back. In psychological terms, we experience temporary changes and then rapidly revert to type. Personal reality is self-sustaining and resistant to alteration.

This is why diets and exercise regimes rarely work, and personal and organizational change programs typically have little impact. All we are doing is moving into a new space for a while, before being pulled back again by the gravity of personal reality. To make deep and long-term improvements to our lives, we need to free ourselves from this gravity field. Although we might make a conscious decision to change, our unconscious mind will pull us back. Any positive force we build will be weaker than the downward force of our unconscious fears and anxieties.

The unconscious mind is like the hidden force in *Groundhog Day* that keeps Phil trapped in repetitive cycles. Phil is locked in two prisons. One is the prison of time, the other the prison of his own reality. It takes him a very long time to understand that it is only when he escapes from the latter, that he can escape from the former.

Our Own Time Trap

This is how the Groundhog Day Effect works. Like Phil, we might be imprisoned in a repetitive cycle of thoughts, feelings, and behaviors over which we believe we have little control. Our reality directs us as though we are characters in a movie, making us stick rigidly to our roles and our lines. You would hardly expect Rita to punch Ned Ryerson or execute a bank robbery; it would be out of character. Similarly, you are playing the part of your character as scripted in your past.

Phil does the best he can with his limited reality. Unknowingly, he creates his own miserable days. He expects to have a bad time and feels undervalued by the people to whom he feels superior. He believes Rita is an inexperienced producer and simply ignores Larry the cameraman. Like a prison cell, his reality isolates him from others.

Five Common Categories of Personal Reality

There are five common categories of personal reality, each distinguished by a specific, overriding need or motivation that creates a distinctive Groundhog Day Effect. Phil's personal reality is complex, yet also shares the characteristics of a more common category.

Entitlement

Phil's reality is dominated by a sense of entitlement. He is trapped in habitual patterns of thoughts and behaviors such as selfishness, pride, and self-centeredness bordering on narcissism. He believes that the more he focuses on satisfying his own needs, the happier he will become. Phil wants everything his own way when he arrives in town. He demands the best hotel and is sarcastic to the hotel manager when she is unable to provide cappuccino or espresso.

The problem is that "entitled" people can never get their needs satisfied. They have repetitive thoughts like "everyone must pay attention to me now" or "the world owes me a living." I once knew a very wealthy lady who was stuck in an endless cycle; her self-esteem was dependent on continually getting what she wanted. Unfortunately, she never had enough. Whatever she looked like or owned, she always felt an underlying lack of self-worth. She had to be stimulated all the time, and hated to be bored or alone for even a moment. She was never able to build intimate relationships because she was too self-centered and insensitive to the needs of others. Lacking genuine connection, she diverted herself by looking for meaning in the instant gratification of activities such as shopping or partying.

Insecurity

Many people have a personal reality dominated by insecurity. I have met many people who suffer from repetitive patterns of low self-esteem, poor self-image, loneliness, and disconnection. They tend to have repetitive thoughts such as "I am not worthy of love" or "I can't make friends" or "I will never be happy." Their behavior reflects this as they are inclined to underachieve and are fearful of forming intimate relationships. They may even prefer to be alone rather than risk being hurt by someone else in a new relationship.

Throughout their lives, insecure people interpret the world as a hostile place, and yearn to run away from difficulties or responsibility. They like to simplify everything and narrow their experiences. Their natural tendency to flee from reality stems from an underlying need to avoid other people so nobody can hurt them.

Dependency

Dependent people fail to develop into fully independent and autonomous adults. They suffer from repetitive patterns of pessimism and lack confidence. They tend to have recurrent thoughts such as "I need someone to look after me" or "I don't like new experiences." They avoid responsibility or risk, which can lead to a life of underperformance. Their natural inclination is to stay in small familiar groups, their "comfort zone," where they can avoid pain.

Unable to find answers themselves, dependent persons are always looking for something or someone else to solve their problems. Often they spend their lives in a fruitless search for the perfect partner who will "complete them."

Even if they believe they have found such a person, the delusion rapidly disappears. Dependent people are unable to cope with the truth that their partner is imperfect and unable to provide them with the meaning and certainty they crave.

Approval

I know of many people who spend their lives overachieving, looking for the approval they never got from their parents. Desperate for attention, they become trapped in repetitive cycles of people pleasing. Recurrent thoughts include "Do they like me or not?" and "I have to be famous, wealthy, or beautiful before anyone will like me."

A personal reality driven by approval and recognition can lead to great success and achievement. The problem is that the cycle never ends, and no amount of approval is ever enough to compensate for the lack of it in childhood. Whatever they achieve, however beautiful they are, and regardless of how much money they make, these people will never be truly happy or find peace of mind. They have based their happiness on what others think of them, and this is always doomed to failure.

Control

We all want and benefit from some degree of control. The difficulty arises with people who have to be in complete control of everything. They have recurring thoughts such as "I have to be perfect in everything I do" or "I am only happy if I am in control." Their high need for control leads to great frustration, as life rarely conforms to their rigid rules, or their craving for consistency, order, and predictability. They seek to control people and events to meet their needs. They want to be invulnerable, though they never can be.

Their reality produces unrealistic expectations and desires. In effect, their world and the real world are in conflict. It is easy for them to believe their childlike illusions that the real world should conform to their personal reality; harder to accept that their filters were wrong and they themselves must change. They are doomed to never-ending disappointment. As we learn as adults, it is impossible for people and events always to turn out the way we want.

I once worked for a manager who was always impatient and frustrated as he tried hard to control the world around him, but to no avail. Nobody could live up to his high expectations, and he never developed empathy with his team. His obsession with control was a doomed attempt to conceal his vulnerability. He could control the finances to an extent, but he could not control either his emotions or other people's. He could never create that perfect world where everyone behaved predictably.

Each type of personal reality separates us from an authentic, fulfilling life; each has its own needs, meanings, and motivations. In effect, each one takes charge of our minds and directs our lives in predictable and generally unhelpful ways. Each reality represents a state of consciousness that we project out on to our external reality, and that dictates the scope and quality of our experience.

Each one creates its own huge gap in our lives, which it can never fill. Ultimately, someone who feels a sense of entitlement or who wants to be in control will always be disappointed. All the types are our minds' best attempt to protect our fragile self-esteem and prevent us from being hurt. Unfortunately, each produces its particular version of the Groundhog Day Effect and prevents us from finding the magic in our lives.

CHAPTER THREE

The Magic of Paying Attention

⌒

The remainder of this book is dedicated to exploring how we can transform our reality and break free of the Groundhog Day Effect. All the clues and all the resources are secrets imbedded in the movie, waiting to be discovered. The same steps that Phil Connors takes to escape the time loop he is stuck in are the steps we can take to escape the Groundhog Day Effect in our lives—and find happiness and fulfillment. This is the magic of the movie.

The title *The Magic of Groundhog Day* refers to the magical personal reality that Phil Connors creates over the course of the movie. It describes how he learns to recognize, experience, and cultivate the magic in everyday life. The *Oxford American Dictionary* defines magic as "an enchanting quality or phenomenon." When we are enchanted with life, we shift our consciousness, and that produces a wonderful feeling of aliveness, joy, hope, and openness to possibilities.

A magical reality creates a state of mind that delights in the magic all around us—in ourselves, in other people, and in nature. We appreciate the gift of life, see the best in others, and discover magic in every moment. What is more magical than the gift of life? What is more magical than the human brain and consciousness? What is more magical than Planet Earth?

Our problem is that our regular personal reality often conceals the magic from us. The magic is always present all around us—in seeing the first buds of spring, in lying on the grass watching the clouds roll by, in listening to Beethoven. It is the magic of loving and being loved, and it is the mystery of life itself, of which we still know so little

Phil's Discovery of Magic

During the movie, Phil finds this magical state by altering the way he experiences the world. When he changes his reality he sees that life on Groundhog Day—on February 2 in Punxsutawney—is perfect as it is. You can live in a magical state if you break free of your restrictive personal reality and experience the real world more directly. When you stop thinking all the time and start paying attention, the magic returns—the same magic that animated your childhood.

There are five types of magic that Phil discovers in the

movie, and each one contributes to a magical personal reality: the magic of paying attention, the magic of repetition, the magic of acceptance, the magic of creativity, and the magic of love. Magic unfolds when we transform our reality by consciously applying these five types of magic to everything we do. Each one enables transformation, preventing the stagnation that results if we allow the Groundhog Day Effect to continue unchecked.

You might then discover that your life is already perfect. What if all you had to do was alter your perspective and become aware of the perfection? What if it is a question of discovering the perfection in your life rather than creating it? This is potentially one of the most powerful insights you could ever have.

The First Step towards Transformation

What if the most important change you had to make was to give up the search for new acquisitions, new places, and new people and simply rediscover that you have it all now? This can happen when you practice the first type of magic: the magic of attention.

Paying attention is the act of consciously choosing where to direct your attention. You pay attention when you are reading the paper, engaging in a fascinating conversation, or watching an engrossing movie. You pay attention when you stop living in the trance of your personal reality and come back to the world as it is. Above all, paying attention is the first step toward transforming your life.

When Phil arrives in Punxsutawney, he is not paying attention to anything other than his own needs. He is there to do a job he does not want to do, and get out of town as quickly as possible. On his first day, he does not notice the people or the events around him. Even his colleagues are only there to help him deal with this inconvenience as best they can. He is in such a rush that he steps into a deep puddle by mistake—and does it again the next day.

He is anxious to stay in the best hotel in town, get to bed early, and avoid any of the town's festivities. This is his fourth Groundhog Day festival and he has probably never participated in any of the events. The place and the celebration are simply the setting to complete an irritating chore, a means to an end. There is no magic here.

Completely focused on his own needs, Phil is paying attention to his anticipated future, not to the present. He is trapped in the Groundhog Day Effect even before he is trapped in Groundhog Day itself. Ironically, it is only by being physically trapped that he is forced to recognize he is psychologically trapped as well. In turn, his physical release requires his psychological liberation.

Repetition Compels Us to Pay Attention

Phil is forced to look beyond his personal reality and become aware of the reality of the world in which he is stuck. Since each day is identical, he can clearly see the results of his behavior. He has to see each day as separate, and think about how he wants to spend it. While he is stuck in his own little selfish world he cannot make the change; when he begins to notice what is going on in Punxsutawney, he moves beyond his self-absorption.

When Phil pays heed to his surroundings, he is able to see the charm and beauty of the small town in front of him. He gradually shifts from being dissatisfied with what he is missing, such as a five-star hotel and sophisticated nightlife, to appreciating what he has, such as the ability to play the piano and help people.

During the time Phil is self-absorbed, he has "tunnel vision." He only sees the nightmare of his predicament. His worldview has led to dissatisfaction rather than gratitude, and he can only see a dull town of boring, inferior people. When he starts to pay attention, he becomes aware of the extraordinary nature of ordinary small-town life. He savors the sequence of daily events, the content of each conversation, and the life story of everyone he meets.

He then recognizes Punxsutawney as a delightful town of decent people who each have their own value. He comes to know the town intimately. He learns the personal stories of the staff and the customers of the local restaurant. He discovers that Doris the waitress dreams of going to Paris before she dies. And that Bill, a waiter for three years, likes the town, paints toy soldiers, and is gay. As he gets to know the locals he finds that, contrary to the popular saying, familiarity breeds affection rather than contempt.

Phil also starts to become aware of his own feelings and develops more self-awareness. His idea of what is important in his life changes dramatically during his time in Punxsutawney. At the beginning of the movie, this self-absorbed prima donna covets wealth, fame, and status: what his personal reality reinforces and craves. By the end, he has discovered that what he really wants is love, meaning, and peace of mind.

Over countless repetitive days, Phil discovers what matters to him most and discerns the difference between satisfying his ego and fulfilling his genuine needs. Like millions of us, Phil has to distinguish between means and ends. He initially wants wealth and fame because he believes these are the means to achieving the end he craves—a sense of love, meaning, and contentment. In the end, Phil finds the direct path to this sense. He discovers that he can bypass all the trivial distractions of minor celebrity and find love and peace of mind by being authentic. By giving up the means, he gets to the end more rapidly and more securely.

Phil has to find happiness in the "doing" of his immediate activities, because there is no future for which to prepare. He has to find happiness now, because "now" is all he has. In the process, he becomes clear about what is important. He learns to distinguish the genuine magic of the world about him from the illusory magic his old personal reality craved.

When We Pay Attention, We Discover Magic

When Phil pays attention, he discovers the magic of Punxsutawney. He learns to love the weather, the Groundhog Day ceremony, and the people. By the end of the movie, he is even planning to stay there and not return to Pittsburgh. What once seemed boring is now fascinating, and what seemed small and trivial is now meaningful. Conversely, what once seemed very important, like fame, now seems irrelevant.

We can learn a great deal by paying attention to Phil. Indirectly, he is acting on our behalf. We want to see him do more and more crazy things. He is like the mischievous boy at school whom the other children goad to play the pranks they are too afraid to do themselves. In many ways, he enacts our own fantasies. Have you wanted to know the future, and use it to manipulate people and events? Have you ever imagined a life of unadulterated pleasure doing whatever you want with no consequences?

There must be more to life than having everything.

MAURICE SENDAK

Such desires are entirely natural, and part of what is often known as our "shadow side." The eminent psychologist Carl Jung believed that we all have a shadow self[1] that reveals our deeper emotions and intentions. In our everyday lives, we learn for the most part to control these thoughts through self-discipline. Phil's actions allow us to witness what happens when our shadow runs the show.

He eats and drinks as much as he wants, amuses himself as much as he wants, and has sex as much as he wants.

He is living the life you might have dreamed of, or might even have led at one time. He symbolizes the fantasy of our consumer culture: you can have whatever you want whenever you want. You can also see that this fantasy is a delusion, for Phil's fantasy turns into a nightmare, as it probably would for you too.

A Permanent Present

Whatever Phil does to amuse and distract himself, he cannot escape the fact that he is facing an eternity of the same day. He has to confront both immortality and the recurrence of the same day forever. His view of time changes, and this helps to change his personal reality.

Phil is caught in an inner time loop created by his past conditioning. He experiences each day through the filter of his reality, which is a frozen snapshot of the past. It needs interpretations of the past to give it meaning. This distorts time, and initially prevents him from being in the present moment. It is only when he escapes time altogether and lives in a permanent present that he can escape this frozen time and see things as they truly are.

During the time loop, Phil radically changes how he conceives of time. At first, time is an *irritation* to be endured, as he waits to return to his former life as a celebrity weatherman in the city. Then time is a *resource,* which he can use to exploit others. Next, it is a terrible *bur-den* to be suffered for eternity. Finally, time is a great *gift*, which he can use to help others and find happiness. Time remains the same; it is Phil's attitude to it that changes.

At first, Phil is only focused on the future, on how he can get out of Punxsutawney. As a weatherman, he is pre-occupied with planning for the future: for the next TV show, the next remote broadcast. His visit on Groundhog Day is an annoying distraction in his busy schedule.

Now, trapped in time, he has no choice but to live in the present moment. He has a past, but it becomes increas-ingly less relevant as he repeats the same day over and over again. Similarly, his future is of little significance, since there are no consequences to his actions beyond the twenty-four hours he inhabits. Phil has to be present in this one day, because that is all he has. This one day *is his life*. There is no tomorrow.

When Phil discards the trivial, he learns to spend his day wisely. He has no choice because the trivial no longer satisfies him. His personal reality is starting to collapse; there is no past or future to maintain its structure. His future has literally been taken away from him, and his new sense of time profoundly influences his personal reality. By the end of the movie, he does not waste his day in regret about the past or anxiety about the future. By being firmly in the present, he accomplishes an extraordinary amount, and is far happier.

A Turning Point

By the end of *Groundhog Day*, Phil no longer looks to the future. He no longer focuses on how life might be, because that choice has been taken from him. He no longer believes he will only be happy when he has left town, or when he has won the big job promotion. Indeed, it is only when the future has been removed that he can recognize the gift of the present. What seems dreadful is in fact magical. He tells Rita, *"No matter what happens, tomorrow or for the rest of my life, I'm happy now because I love you."*

This is a pivotal stage in the movie. Phil is happy with the present moment, with life as it is, not as it might be or should be. Phil has become conscious by living in the moment and paying attention. His senses are open and he savors each moment. When you learn to do the same, you will be happier too.[2]

Eventually, Phil stops searching for a means to escape and is happy just being in Punxsutawney with Rita. The town was never the problem; his perspective was. Once he pays attention to the town and learns to make the most of the present moment, he discovers the magic. You can do the same. You just need to open your eyes and see the world around you.

Escaping Automatic Pilot

When we suffer from Groundhog Day Effect, we forget that we are on automatic pilot. Trapped by routine, we rush through each day in predetermined activities, like working or parenting or going to school. The routine dictates how we live, and the routine suppresses our ability to be aware.

One of the chief reasons we are trapped in our own Groundhog Day is that we are not paying attention. How much of your life is a means to an end, a set of tasks to perform, and a routine to get through? Are you paying more attention to your personal reality than to the outer world? Do you find that you are continually lost in thought, and that even when you are with someone else, you rarely engage with them, listening only to yourself?

Walk down a busy street and notice how many of the people you pass seem to be lost in their own Groundhog Day. Does it seem that others are in a hurry, doing more and more in less time? The demands for greater productivity and multitasking are speeding up everything, and intensifying the Groundhog Day Effect. We are too busy to be conscious of the world about us. We are living in a trance.

I know of many people and many organizations that function this way. They are preoccupied with increasing the *quantity* of what they do at the expense of the *quality* of their experience. I know of executives who sleep-walk through their days, under the illusion that they are improving their performance by doing more—when in fact they are achieving the opposite. Lost in the details of their mindless daily routine, they miss the big picture; they have no vision to inspire and lead their people.

Only self-awareness can lead to genuine personal and

organizational change. For when you pay attention to the present moment rather than your thoughts, and to the world rather than your personal reality, you gain the awareness to see things more clearly. You begin to notice again that the world around you is magical. You knew this as a child. When you were very young and possessed what Buddhists call a "beginner's mind," you were able to perceive magic everywhere—in the feel of the wind, the flight of a bee, and the beauty of your mother's smile. As you have grown older, you have forgotten and disconnected yourself from the magic.

Is it so small a thing
To have enjoy'd
the sun,
To have lived light in
the spring,
To have loved,
to have thought,
to have done . . .

MATTHEW ARNOLD

As our personal reality hardens with age and conditioning, we fall prey to the Groundhog Day Effect. We progressively lose our ability to pay attention and experience magic. We become preoccupied with our plans, routines, and everyday concerns. Often we take things and people for granted, as so frequently happens in marriages and long-term friendships.

Life continues to be amazing; it always has been. It is just that we have stopped noticing. Sometimes we might awaken for a moment and stand in awe at a beautiful sunset, although such rare moments do little to shake most of us out of our sleepwalking.

Learning to Attend

When you are trapped in the Groundhog Day Effect, you can lose hope. When you pay attention, you start to rediscover hope. When you pay attention every day to the magic of life, you remind yourself of the gift of life and the gift of consciousness. You also start to observe, challenge, and undermine your unhealthy personal reality. You take charge of your thoughts and discover a more enlightened and magical way of experiencing life.

This can be very hard. At work, at school, and at home we are hypnotized by the compulsive need to fill every moment with activities. Nowhere is this more worrying than with respect to our children. I remember a family in the United Kingdom where the parents organized every minute of their children's' lives like a military campaign. Overscheduled and overstimulated, these poor youngsters were caught in an activity trap, living at a frenetic pace with no room for quiet, unstructured time. Under constant pressure, poor at concentration, and uncomfortable with their own company, they suffered from chronic stress and anxiety. We could all benefit from slowing down and doing less. When we pay attention more often and for longer periods of time we weaken the shackles of the Groundhog Day Effect. This means paying attention to the present moment, paying attention to what is going on around us, and paying attention to each other.

Like Phil, when we are aware of your feelings, we continue to break through the personal reality that has frozen our emotions for so long. We experience more emotions and we experience them more fully. Such self-awareness also enables us to recognize and interrupt repetitive thought and behavior patterns that were previously automatic and unconscious.

The first step to paying attention is to become conscious of being on automatic pilot. Then we can begin to observe how our minds works. For example, if you are sitting at your desk in the office, notice how many times you are doing one thing while thinking about something else. When you are in a dull meeting, observe how you "switch off" as your mind wanders. Bring your attention back to the moment and stay with it.

I once coached a salesperson who was a brilliant networker. She was great at opening sales but very poor at closing them. I taught her to maintain her focus, not to think about other sales prospects or what might go wrong, and simply complete the steps leading to the sale. She learned to manage her mind, stop herself drifting off, and stick to her plan. This led to a massive increase in her sales.

So when you are feeling anxious, consciously observe the sequence of perception, thought, and emotion. You will be able to see past the object of your anxiety to how you are making yourself anxious. As you allow yourself to fully feel the anxiety, you are better able to release it. This is preferable to trying to suppress the feeling.

When you pay attention, you also start to appreciate life more. Indeed, our inability as humans to be grateful for what we have is possibly the most important limitation in our lives—and one of the most serious blocks to our happiness. Throughout history, every type of culture has celebrated the gift of life. Modern Western society is the exception. We spend far more time complaining and bemoaning our fate than we do expressing thankfulness. We might say grace before meals, but we have few other regular rituals for celebrating life.

> *I hate ingratitude more in a man than lying, vainness, babbling, drunkenness, or any taint of vice whose strong corruption inhabits our frail blood.*
>
> WILLIAM SHAKESPEARE,
> *TWELFTH NIGHT*

Constrained by the Groundhog Day Effect, even our good experiences become habit. We exist on automatic pilot, forgetting all the good things in our lives, always searching for what we lack. Unfortunately, our buy-more, do-more culture keeps us locked in a continuous state of ingratitude.

What Are You Paying Attention To?

Modern consumer society depends on our perpetual dissatisfaction. When we are dissatisfied, we buy products to help fill the gap. Because a purchase never does fill the gap for more than a passing moment, we become ensnared in a never-ending cycle of dissatisfaction and consumerism. Just turn on the TV and watch the commercials for fitness equipment, diet pills, and baldness cures. Thousands of commercials have one message: you will only be happy when you have bought this product.

Do you pay the most attention to what you do not have? Are you unhappy with how much you earn, how you look, what you have achieved, and what is missing in your life? Where is your focus? From magazines and media, to education and the workplace, everything is a race for more beauty, status, fame, and wealth. Phil believes he will be happy when he becomes a weatherman at a bigger television network. What do you believe you are missing?

Whatever you think you are missing, be forewarned that when you start this race, you commit yourself to permanent frustration and discontent. Even if you are the one in ten thousand who is beautiful, wealthy, powerful, and famous, you will still want more or be worried about losing what you have. You are on a treadmill you can never get off.

I remember meeting an older multimillionaire on vacation a few years ago. He had been poor and achieved great financial success, which made him happy for a while. Then, bored with his wealth, he divorced his wife and dated a succession of younger women in search of this elusive happiness. Bored with sex, he turned his attention to his health and spent a fortune on plastic surgery and anti-aging treatments. When that failed to do it, he became obsessed with death, veering from one religion and New Age movement to another. I expect he is still searching.

Like this lost soul, many of us are so exhausted from chasing the shadows of our cravings that we cannot see the light around us. We are so fixated on the clouds passing by that we do not see that the sun is always there just behind.

Whenever you feel dissatisfied or resentful, think about the magic of being born. The odds of being born at all are like winning every lottery in the world every day, for the whole of your life. The chance of your parents meeting, having sex, and the particular sperm from your father fertilizing your mother's egg is many billions to one. Then think of the chance of the same thing happening to their sets of parents. This raises the odds of your being born to trillions to one. Now go back through the thousands of generations of your ancestors. There is no number to come even close to how unlikely your birth was!

Do you ever think about this amazing phenomenon of coincidence? In contrast, how many times have you thought about what is wrong with your life—all the things you don't have and all the injustices done to you? Have you forgotten the miracle of your own birth, the magic of your existence? Is it time to remember?

What greater magic is there than being alive? What greater magic is there than awakening to the beauty around you? *Groundhog Day* might be magical, yet there is a greater magic still in your life. You can discover magic in your life because life *is* magical. All you need to do is pay attention.

This sounds too simple. Surely, there must be a catch?

Doesn't it take a lot of hard work to be happy? Well, yes it does. It takes a lot of hard work to let go of the irrational belief that happiness is achieved through getting everything you thought you wanted.

Five Steps to Happiness Through Paying Attention

The simple act of paying attention is the most direct route to happiness, and there are five steps that will lead you there when you take them day by day.

Step One—A Sense of Gratitude

Remind yourself every day of your good fortune. Start by considering the gift of life. Slow down and take time to appreciate the small details. You will gain so much. You will save a fortune in time and money when you break free from the distractions of consumerism. You will prevent enormous stress and loss of energy. And you will achieve a more secure, longer-lasting state of well-being.

> *A short cut to riches is to subtract from our desires.*
>
> FRANCESCO PETRARCH

A sense of gratitude is one of the most important characteristics of happy people. Martin Seligman, the psychologist at the forefront of the positive psychology movement, has developed a range of tools for promoting gratitude. These include keeping a journal of what makes you happy, and seeking out people who have helped you and thanking them directly[3]

If you want to be happy, pay much more attention to what you already have and forget about what you don't have. Like Phil, you will appreciate that you have what you need right here and right now. Even the most happy, balanced, and well-adjusted people can benefit from cultivating a sense of gratitude. This is the most practical and achievable advice I have been given, or could ever give.

Step Two—Self-Awareness
When you are mindful, you also become more aware of yourself. You become aware that you are stuck in the Groundhog Day Effect. You are able to see the truth of your situation, and understand why you are stuck. You will probably blame someone or something else at first. When you look deeper, you will see that the cause is not the world, but your worldview.

You become more self-aware. You see that you are more than your personal reality, more than your thoughts, more than your beliefs, more than your emotions, more than your possessions and achievements. You are much more than the sum of these parts to which you have become so attached.

When you pay attention, you are able to see that your personality and self-image are insubstantial and illusory. As you awaken from your trance, you regain consciousness and see how your patterns determine your life. You see that you are not your patterns. You recognize that you created these patterns, and that you can alter them too.

This can be painful, as you might have to let go of cherished illusions you have about yourself, and admit your true intentions. Until you can get closer to the truth about yourself, rather than the illusion created by your reality, you will remain stuck.

You are confronting your shadow. The shadow is not only important to the groundhog it is also important to you. Your personal reality casts a shadow that you carry with you. Once you pay attention to your shadow, you can begin to see your authentic self rather than your imagined one.

When you pay attention to your feelings, you can bring deep emotions to the surface. This can be a powerful, even traumatic experience. Many people keep their feelings buried. They are like a closed flower that never blooms. By trying to stay safe and secure in their comfort zone, they shut themselves off from the full spectrum of emotions.

Step Three—Identify What Is Important

Paying attention also helps you to become clearer about what is important in your life, and to establish what it is you really want. How much of your life have you spent devoted to the "means" and how much have you spent enjoying the "ends"? How much of your life have you spent delaying your happiness until circumstances were perfect? If you focus on the means, you will have few moments of happiness. If you focus on the ends, you will have a lifetime full of such moments

If you want to be happy, find work and friends that make you happy now. Have fun in the performance of your job and in the time you spend with friends. If you want peace of mind, be peaceful now. Don't wait until all the circumstances are ideal.

Magical movies like *Groundhog Day* strike a chord deep within us because we intuitively believe there is a better life for us out there; we want to experience the same magic as our favorite movie characters. Fortunately, you do not need to wait for wizards to wave their wands and give you what you think you want. You are the magician and you have the magic to create your own spells. You find the magic when you break free of your own Groundhog Day and pay attention to what you really want.

Ultimately, we all want the feeling of loving and being loved, the feeling of security and inner peace, the feeling of having a greater purpose. We want a state of mind or a particular feeling more than the specific achievement, or possession, that we believe will produce the feeling.

When you pay attention, you also shed a powerful light that exposes the facade of your personal reality and helps to free you from the Groundhog Day Effect. You discern how your patterns work and observe your compulsive thinking. When you monitor your thoughts like this, you can start to change them. You move from unconscious, habitual, and automatic thinking to conscious thinking. You choose where to focus attention rather than letting your habitual patterns of thought decide. Maintaining such moment-to-moment awareness is critical to changing your reality.

Paying attention is demanding. As I described earlier, your mind is a work-shy "cognitive miser." It copes with your fast-moving, complex, and busy lifestyle by taking short cuts. These get you through the hundreds of emails, phone calls, and routine duties that make up your day. Yet despite all these pressures, you can still choose where to focus your attention moment to moment. You can interrupt negative patterns of thoughts and bring your attention back to where you want it to be.

When you observe your moods and feelings, you notice that they are separate and transient. This weakens their hold on you. If you have a cold, you do not believe you *are* the cold. You separate yourself from your illness. You see that you have a cold, you treat it, and know that it will pass. You can learn to do the same for unhealthy thoughts, emotions, and moods. Just as you do not say "I am the cold" you do not say "I am an unhappy person." Moreover, you did not give yourself a bad cold, but you did give yourself the bad thought. You are in charge here.

Step Four — Be Mindful
This form of observation and understanding is often referred to as "mindfulness," which is a Buddhist practice

for being aware of your thoughts and behaviors in the present moment.[4] When you are mindful, you pay attention to what is happening in your mind and in the world around you. The aim is meditative, to rise above your thoughts and not be lost in the process of thinking. This enables you to shift among different ways of thinking and experiencing the world rather than being stuck in the same recurrent patterns.

You are paying attention when you interrupt your trance. Say you are walking down the street and you think you hear someone shout your name. You immediately turn your attention to the present—even if they are calling for someone else. Similarly, facing a crisis— such as finding out you are seriously ill or losing your job—will lift you out of your routine.

The problem is that this type of attention to the present moment is reactive. How do you voluntarily pay attention more often and at the right time? The answer is to find a way of breaking down the daily patterns of automatic behavior, the Groundhog Day Effect.

Step Five—Slow Down

One idea is to change speed. You disrupt automatic patterns when you slow down. This is because so much of what you do is at high speed. When you are stuck in the Groundhog Day Effect your habits take over and you multitask. You can be composing an email while having a hands-free telephone conversation while making notes for your next meeting while looking around at your colleagues. You are working at such a frenetic pace that you have to rely on short cuts and habitual patterns just to get through the day. Moreover, the faster you live, the stronger the Groundhog Day Effect becomes.

When you slow down, you move out of the high-speed autopilot mode and focus on what is going on around you rather than playing out what is going on in your head. When you go on vacation, you slow down. Typically, you continue in work mode for the first few days and then, as you slow down, you think and feel differently. You are more aware of your body, of other people, and of your surroundings.

Phil's time in Punxsutawney is similar to the times when you go to unfamiliar places. Often, at first, you may not like the strange surroundings, the unusual sights, sounds, and smells. You miss your home comforts and amenities. For a few days, this feeling of dislocation is challenging and unnerving. Then as you gradually awaken from your daily trance, you start to pay attention and enjoy the new sensations. You are slowing down.

When you slow down, you can feel your stress dissolve as you go with the flow. As you become more relaxed, you realize how tense and tight you were when you arrived. You had become habituated to your restlessness as though it was your normal state.

The same happens when you are ill and forced to stay in

bed. After some initial resistance, you have to accept your situation and naturally slow down. Then your mind and body can relax and heal.

Fortunately, you can bring this relaxed holiday mood into your life whenever and wherever you want. You just need to slow down. Walk more slowly and talk more slowly. Take time for meals and find hobbies that absorb you. Plan a hike every weekend so that you can take time to pay attention to nature.

You can also slow down in your town or city, and get to know it as Phil got to know Punxsutawney. A great exercise is to walk at a leisurely pace around your neighborhood and observe the houses, the gardens, and the people whom you encounter. Stop thinking and start experiencing the world instead.

When you slow down, you also start to experience time differently. You can pay attention to how much of your day is spent thinking about the past or the future. This clears the ground for one of the most important skills you can develop: paying attention to the present moment and letting go of the past and future.

How Do You View the Concept of Time?

What if you were to treat today as the only day of your life? What would you do differently? Do you see today as just another twenty-four hours in a long sequence of days that all seem to merge into one another? Or as a precious gift to be cherished? I hope that today is not the only day of your life. I also hope that you will pay attention to how you spend it.

How do you perceive time? Do you believe you are in a frantic race against time, to get everything done within a fixed period? Is time something to be overcome, or is it to be endured? Do you see it as the building block to construct your perfect life *sometime in the future*? Or do you see time as a series of *present moments* to be experienced and savored? Do you want to control time or dance with it? Is the present moment a means to an end or an end in itself?

We are so thoughtless, that we wander through the hours which are not here, regardless only of the moment that is actually our own.

BLAIRE PASCAL

It helps to bring your attention back to the present. When you have a tough task to perform, focus on the doing of the task not on the past- and future-related thoughts you have about it. This can be hard because the future structures and dictates almost everything we do.

Indeed, you might feel that you would fall to pieces if the future were taken away from you and you were forced to continuously repeat the same day. You might feel that there would be no point in doing anything, no purpose, and nothing to strive for. This is how many depressed people feel: that they do not have a future. Phil had no future. He had to reinvent himself.

We live in a world dominated by time—we can never

beat or control time. Constant multitasking and the rush from one activity to another and reveal a person who is trying to be as productive as possible. A person who is continually fixing problems to get through the day, but rarely enjoying the journey.

Time is the organizing principle of our lives. It is the structure of our personal reality. Time also seems to go at different speeds. When you are bored it seems slow. When you are excited or engaged it seems to go much faster. If you have little moment-to-moment awareness, time seems to pass you by. How time flies!

Many people take their days for granted. The days quietly slip by, turning into weeks, months, and years. Days slip by when you are "living in your head." You go to sleep each night and wake up consumed by thoughts, rarely thinking about the day that you are living through other than as a series of activities, a series of tasks to move you forward to tomorrow.

We live in a world structured by time, where so much of what we do is geared toward creating a future. Do you spend your days working and living for a future? Do you work to buy a bigger house, a better car, to pay for your children's education, to finance your retirement?

This does not mean you should pay no attention to the future. Phil does not need to worry about his health, his finances, or his future at all. So he eats and drinks to excess with no thoughts for the consequences. You benefit from finding a balance. Devoting all your time to working to buy a luxury car might be a waste of your present; spending a few hours a week exercising to keep in shape so you live a longer and healthier life is not.

Like Phil, you will progress on your journey to a magical day by paying attention to the world around you. When you do this, you can observe your repetitive patterns come and go. This helps to put you back in charge of your life. You become the master of your mind, not the victim of habitual patterns. Where you choose to mindfully place your attention determines the focus your energy and thoughts. Where you choose to consciously place your attention ultimately determines how happy you are.

CHAPTER FOUR

The Magic of Repetition

⌒

When Phil pays attention, he stops living on automatic pilot. He begins to notice and learn from the constant repetition of the same day. Whereas each day might *feel* the same to us, it *is* exactly the same for Phil. The exact repetitions create a unique and magical setting for Phil to learn about himself, other people, and the world around him. *Groundhog Day* offers us such profound insight into the human condition precisely because Phil lives the same day again and again. He is forced to change himself because nothing else changes. His experience reveals the paradox of repetition. The recurring day both imprisons and liberates him. Over time Phil learns that, rather than being a punishment, repetition is magical and essential to his transformation.

The repetition is magical because it enables Phil to

transform himself, once he recognizes the importance of a single day as a distinct and separate period of time. Because is life consists of an endless repetition of February 2, this day effectively becomes his life. Consequently, each moment takes on greater importance. If we want to transform our lives, we need to fully understand this point. Though we may not be literally

> *Repetition is the Mother of Learning.*
>
> ANONYMOUS

stuck in a cycle of repeating time, each and every moment of our lives is important and offers us an opportunity for change and enjoyment.

Phil's outer world is stuck in time, but so is his inner world. It is only when his outer world stops progressing that he becomes aware of his own inner stagnation. Phil is also stuck in the same location. He cannot leave Punx- sutawney because of the blizzard. His stay there is similar to a retreat, out of time and out of the world. This is a unique opportunity; he learns more from repeating the same experiences on the same day than he would from multiple new experiences.

Phil also interacts with the same people. Every day he converses with Mrs. Lancaster, Ned Ryerson, Rita, and Larry. Every day he has to broadcast from the Groundhog Day ceremony and see the same people at the town square, hotel, and restaurant. In *Groundhog Day*, the time loop forces Phil to confront a unique challenge: how can he make the most of an eternity of the same day? In other words, how does he come to grips with immortality?

He cannot change the external world in any way at all. The day remains the same, the town remains the same, people remain the same, and their behavior remains the same. These clear, fixed, repetitive boundaries intensify the focus on Phil, shining a fierce spotlight on everything he does. He tries to control the world until he is forced to see the futility of this strategy. Then he focuses all his attention on changing the one thing he can change—his reaction to the world.

The Lesson of the Time Loop

Phil has to consider all his options and find an answer to the challenge of getting past February 2. When he first realizes that the day is repeating, his reaction is shock, He focuses on finding a way to cope with his predicament. Only later on does he consider that the time loop can be an amazing opportunity for growth.

The repetitions have a cumulative effect on Phil. At first, his old personal reality makes him deny and fear the time loop, but then he starts to exploit it. Because he is selfish, he uses the repetitions selfishly. He bolsters his reality and pushes it as far as it will go. He reverts to adolescent behavior, and like an irritating teenager shows how clever he is at every opportunity. His unique foreknowledge of the daily recurrences enables him to have fun with them.

Knowing in advance what everyone is going to say and do, at breakfast he answers all of the hotel owner's questions before she has a chance to ask them.

For most of the time, Phil lives as though there are no consequences, since he wakes up every morning with nothing altered. Each day, all of the previous days' events are wiped clean—none of the townspeople remember anything that happened. So he can get drunk, get arrested, punch Ned Ryerson, and forget to floss without any consequences at all. He is living every teenager's fantasy. He can do whatever he wants without inhibition or accountability, like an irresponsible business that pollutes its environment without any care for the impact of its activities.

The problem is that this strategy is simply a diversion. Phil spends many hundreds of days choosing the same repetitive thoughts and behaviors until they stop working. He exhausts all the possibilities of a particular activity, like robbing the bank truck, until he becomes completely bored with it. Now the repetition becomes his master, not his servant. He learns the limits of his old reality, as it stops serving him under the exaggerated conditions of extreme repetition.

By repeating activities so many times, he is able to distinguish between what is genuinely worthwhile and what is not. Like a bell curve, he increases his pleasure for a while, reaches a peak, and then experiences rapidly diminishing returns. Even the gratification of seducing local women like Nancy wears off after a while.

Phil begins to realize that there are consequences to his actions. He can make a positive difference to other people during the twenty-four hours of each February 2. Once he appreciates that there are consequences to his actions, he is able to evaluate and modify his behavior. Eventually, he uses the repetitions to help others rather than exploit them. This leads him to change his inner life, even if he can't change his outer life.

Phil would not have changed at all if he had left Punxsutawney without the time loop occurring. He would have continued on his career path, unaware that he was trapped in a personal reality dominated by entitlement and selfishness. His wealth and fame would have disguised the meaninglessness of his life, and the gravity field of his reality would have kept him at its own lower, narrower level of experience.

It is only the repetition that shoves everything in his face, making him aware of the limits of his reality. He begins to see that his old attitudes, thoughts, and behaviors no longer work. He cannot hide from this anymore because the diversions stop working too.

The endless recurrences enable Phil to experiment each day with a new approach to life, and then measure the results. Every morning when he wakes up, he knows that the conditions are exactly the same for his experiment. So he can compare the results of each daily approach he takes.

The experiment is replicable, measurable, and testable. Phil can measure the effect of changing just one variable. If

all he does is change the way he greets Larry the cameraman in the morning, he can measure the results of that single modification. He can monitor and improve his
performance by closely observing what happens to him,
and the other people around him, as he tries new ideas.

Seeing Phil trapped in time reveals the repetitious
nature of life in general. It might be that repetition is the
nature of our existence, and we—as individuals and as
societies—can never escape certain cycles or loops. Maybe
Phil is caught in a whole series of time loops. Before he
arrives in Punxsutawney he is already caught in the loop of
his job as a weatherman. Then he is literally trapped in
time. And then he moves to the new loop of falling in love
with Rita.

Some Loops Are Positive

Perhaps the more important point is to appreciate that we
will always be in a loop, and that we should consider which
loop we want to be in. There are good loops to be in, where
we can use repetition to our advantage. Many routines are
essential. We all need regular food, exercise, and sleep. We
need regular income and benefit greatly from frequent
contact with family and friends. Whether at school, work,
or home, we all need to repeat certain activities.

Routine is the foundation of health, well-being, and
success. The most successful people in the world have regular habits. Top sports people and musicians have to prac-

tice and repeat basic skills and techniques all the time. Phil only becomes an accomplished pianist through an enormous amount of hard, repetitive practice. His improved performance is one of the best clues to just how long he spends in the time loop.

Routines and habits also provide a familiar structure and certainty to our lives that are very comforting. My late father was very content in his routine. In his retirement he would get up every morning at seven a.m., make a cup of tea, and walk to the shops to buy a newspaper at eight. At nine, he would go to his study and paint for two hours. At eleven, he would have a cup of coffee and then paint again until one p.m. The afternoon would follow a similar pattern. Then he would have dinner at half past six, read for a few hours, watch the nine o'clock evening news, have a coffee, and retire to bed.

I used to chide my father for his rigid routine, as I thought it was excruciatingly boring. My life was fast-moving and exciting. I traveled frequently between the United Kingdom and the United States, while my father never left the small town where he lived, daily repeating the same choreographed movements.

I was enjoying great success in business while Dad was stuck in seeming monotony. Now as I write these words, five years after his death, I realize that we were both stuck in repetitive loops. The difference was that he enjoyed his more than I did mine.

I might have been traveling the world, staying in five-star hotels, and driving luxury cars, but I was not particularly happy. I was rushing around in circles searching in vain for meaning and satisfaction. I was suffering from the Groundhog Day Effect. I just couldn't see it.

Dad made repetition work for him. He loved the consistency and familiarity of his routine. In part, it contrasted with the chaos and uncertainty of five dangerous years in the navy during World War II. He chose his routine because he enjoyed what he was doing. I chose my routine because I believed that was how a successful entrepreneur was supposed to live. In essence, I was living in someone else's loop. Everything I did was intended to project an image or live up to an expectation.

I also lacked the pleasure of rituals, which are another example of a positive repetition. They are symbolic acts we perform at regular intervals, such as saying grace, watching the sunset, or celebrating Thanksgiving and Yom Kippur. Or they can be more spontaneous, such as listening to a particular piece of music when you want inspiration, or reading a favorite poem at the end of a difficult day.

Rituals tend to be positive and comforting repetitions that remind us of what is important. They often connect us to hundreds of years of tradition, to others in our family, and our wider circle as well. When we perform rituals, such as lighting a candle or saying grace, we are improving the quality of the moment, and imparting meaning to our daily life.

Rituals are deliberate, conscious repetitions that contrast the unconscious repetitions in our lives. Most of us tend to avoid repetition because we think it is boring.

Instead we distract ourselves. We long for variety and change which, paradoxically, can keep us stuck. The more we divert ourselves, the less aware we are of the deeper patterns of our lives. It is repetition that makes these patterns visible.

When we look at the patterns we see that our realities have created powerful recurring loops. These loops can be both short or long term, and they drive what we do. For example, if you have a reality based on insecurity you will be caught in short-term loops such as automatically backing down from arguments, finding it difficult to be assertive, or saying no to people. Then you might also be caught in larger, long-term loops such as an undemanding career or a debilitating relationship.

Indeed, you can learn a great deal from repetition. If you feel stuck in a particular place, why not try looking at it from a new perspective and take time to make changes in your normal surroundings? You do not need to make a pilgrimage to a faraway land to find the answers to life. They are here in front of you. Like Phil, you can learn more by going deeper into your current experience rather than by going broader.

By repeatedly studying your own surroundings rather than seeking new places, you gain fresh knowledge from the familiar. You change from within rather from without because the "without" is unchanging. Like Phil, you change when you focus less on your external circumstances and more on your inner life.

Do you also tend to see the same people every day—

your family, your colleagues and your friends? You might believe that you need to meet lots of new people to change, but the opposite may be true. When you vary your attitudes and behavior to the same people who form your family and social circle, you are following Phil's path. And the better you get to know your friends and neighbors, the more likely you are to care for them.

In the hope of reaching the moon men fail to see the flowers that blossom at their feet.

ALBERT SCHWEITZER

Remember the five personal realities discussed earlier? If we persevere while being stuck in the Groundhog Day Effect, we can start to recognize our dominating personal reality at work. We can see what is beneficial and what is not. Like Phil, once we concentrate on each day as the building block of our lives, we can intensify our focus, and hopefully improve the quality of our daily experience.

There are many repetitive elements in our lives to learn from, such as commuting or eating our meals or regular meetings at work. Repetition is a permanent, unavoidable mirror that brings everything about us and our lives into sharp focus.

Apply Phil's Experience to Your Life

If you want to replicate the magic of the *Groundhog Day* in your life, imagine what it was like to be Phil Connors. Imagine that you are faced with an eternally recurring day in a place you dislike, with people you despise. What would you do? Would you be exhilarated or depressed? Learn new skills? Or just carry on as you are, hoping for things to get better?

Now think of where you are today. How are you going to spend your day? If you are experiencing the Groundhog Day Effect, you are also facing a form of recurring day. You do not have to be trapped in Punxsutawney to feel that your life is repetitive.

All life is an experiment. The more experiments you make the better.

RALPH WALDO EMERSON

You can replicate the key parts of this experiment in your own life. At first glance it seems to depend on conditions impossible to replicate, such as the time loop. Yet if you see the time loop as metaphorical rather than literal, it is possible to re-create the most important elements of his learning experience for yourself.

Your life might not have the exact characteristics of scientific research, but you can approximate Phil's experience. You can measure the effects of changing your behavior by listening to your partner or not judging your boss for a day. You can even keep a journal to record the experiment and the results.

Of course, there are more variables in our lives than in Phil's, and nothing is static, day to day, the way it is in Punxsutawney. Yet there is a high probability that you will spend tomorrow in the same place and with the same people as today. Most of these people will not be particularly different in their personalities and behavior from today. Each day is a learning opportunity to vary your response to the repetition.

Every day you face multiple choices. Like Phil, you may choose different ways of thinking and behaving. You can spend a month making a conscious effort to be more optimistic or more patient. Choose a behavior that will help you break free of your particular type of reality, and pay special attention to recurring patterns, irritations, or roadblocks. Then record your observations as you develop a scientific approach to your life. Monitoring and understanding your reality is the first step to changing it.

You might notice that people don't respond any differently to you at first. They are not engaged in a similar experiment, and will still put you in the same old box—as you did to them. They might be trapped in their own Groundhog Day.

The only man who behaved sensibly was my tailor; he took my measurement anew every time he saw me, while all the rest went on with their old measurements and expected them to fit me.

GEORGE BERNARD SHAW

Your personal reality is always interacting with that of other people. You see others through the lens of your reality, which is based on the past not the present. Once you start to think this way, you expand your the field of vision to see the subtle patterns that govern so much of what we do.

Experimenting in this way is similar to "action research," the practice of observing yourself in action and learning by doing. When you learn by doing, you closely observe your thinking and behavior, and experiment with different variations. You also apply the same method to others, and see the dynamics in the interplay of different personal realities.[1]

You see that you are part of a system, and that you are almost always in a loop. Then you might consider that if everything is a loop you will need to decide which loop you want to be in—loops that lead to positive results or those that lead to counterproductive results. You can make repetition work for you by replacing negative loops and bad habits with positive ones. Perhaps good repetitions are the foundation of the good life.

Choose What Is Worth Repeating

Every day you have the choice of creating recurrent loops. You can spend an hour each evening watching reality TV and eating pizza, or you could spend the same hour in the gym. You can spend an hour in the bar complaining about how unfair life is, or you could spend the same hour attending a course on entrepreneurship.

I don't know what is right for you. What I do know is that our daily repetitive behaviors create habits by stealth which, as we have seen, form and strengthen our personal reality. Unhealthy habits can easily turn into vicious circles, loops that become increasingly worse.

Our personal reality has its own field of gravity, and as a loop becomes stronger, so does its gravitational force. The effort needed to change then needs to be that much greater. For instance, every time you don't exercise you become less fit, and have less energy to get you to the gym in the first place.

So why not try developing a "virtuous circle" instead. Simply making small adjustments in your daily activities can build large changes over time. For example, when you go hiking you will feel better and have more energy, which is more likely to get you back on the trail. After a few months, the habit is formed and is more likely to continue.

Similarly, I have helped shift businesses from vicious to virtuous circles. Some years ago, I worked with a major media group that was suffering from low morale caused by the falling sales of their flagship newspaper. They had spent a fortune on consultants to design new strategies and a new layout for the paper. Nothing worked, and the harder they tried to change the worse morale got. It was only when we focused on their specific habits and thinking patterns that they were able to break free of the old limiting circle and create a new, positive one, day by day.

Sometimes we do not even need to create a positive loop, since it is already there for us. Breathing is the ultimate example of a beneficial repetition. We can ignore our breath, or become aware of it to our advantage through the practice of meditation.

Repetition can work for us and against us. The key is to know the difference between what works and what does not work. Which repetitions we can change and those we cannot. Then we can practice the magic of acceptance, the subject of our next chapter.

CHAPTER FIVE

The Magic of Acceptance

⌒

E very day on his way to work, Phil passes an old man who is begging for money. At first, Phil does not notice him. Then he ignores him or pretends he has no money to give him. Finally, Phil gives the old man some money and tries to help him.

Phil has recognized that he can use the repetition for good;. Now he wants to use his amazing powers to help others, so he puts all his energies into helping the old man. Unfortunately, the old man is homeless and very ill. Later that night he dies, but Phil is unable to accept his death. He tries to get the man's medical details from the nurse in order to find a cure, while providing food and care, in a desperate attempt to save him.

No matter what Phil does, he cannot save the old When the nurse says that sometimes people just die he replies,

"Not today." Fixing problems had always given Phil a sense of closure and achievement. The dilemma is that although he can fix a quiz show, he cannot fix the problems that count. He has to accept that he cannot save the old man.

For the first time in his life, Phil appreciates suffering. He has had to endure the trauma of being trapped for years in Punxsutawney. He has been torn apart emotionally, suffered a breakdown, and for a while given up on life. Phil in turn opens up to the suffering of others. He accepts that suffering is a necessary part of life, and that the townspeople are fellow human beings who suffer just as he does. This is a revelation. Until now he had been cushioned from the harsh realities of life by his career in the gilded cage of television.

Indeed, this is a major turning point in the story and in Phil's process of change. His acceptance of the true nature of his predicament and the nature of life, with all its pain, triggers the collapse of his old personal reality. He has hit rock bottom and there is nowhere else to go. Though unable to kill his "physical" self, he does kill his old "psychological" self. His personal reality has been annihilated. His beliefs, thoughts, and behaviors were simply not up to the job.

Accepting a New Reality

In the Punxsutawney experiment, the old Phil's reality is exposed as flawed and unsustainable. The structure of his previous fast-paced media lifestyle collapses to reveal his character deficiencies. Phil has had to see himself as he truly is, stripped of his status and supports. His tactics of diversion and exploitation fail completely. Like a balloon, he expands his reality as far as it can go, and it bursts. By reaching the limits of his old life he discovers a new one.

As Phil begins to discover the magic of paying attention and repetition, he begins to accept the truth of his predicament. He must accept that he cannot escape from Groundhog Day or Punxsutawney. Faced with Rita's rejection of his advances, he has to admit that he cannot get everything he wants. He cannot escape from the town, even when he tries to kill himself. He is not God and cannot control everything in his life. In particular, he must accept that he cannot stop the death of the old man.

From Denial to Acceptance

It is obvious that in the beginning of the endlessly repeating day, Phil is not consciously choosing his responses. He is reacting to events as they happen with his conditioned personal reality. He is largely mirroring the classic set of responses to death as described by Elisabeth Kübler-Ross/[1] Her well-known grief model describes the five stages of response that a person experiences when dealing with grief or tragedy: denial, anger, bargaining, depression, and acceptance. Phil works his way through most of these to the stage of acceptance. At this point he finally stops resisting.

In many ways, Phil is grieving for his loss of control and freedom as he faces an eternity in the time loop. When in denial, Phil tries to resist the reality of the time loop and the blizzard that keeps him in Punxsutawney. He is confused and tries to escape. Later he seeks help from his producer, Rita, then a cure from a doctor and psychiatrist.

Phil does not want to accept the time loop. He displaces his fears through a series of diversions like planning a bank robbery and seducing local women. By preoccupying himself with amusing ways of exploiting the time loop, he avoids confronting the overwhelming implications of eternity and immortality.

His personal reality is ill-equipped to handle the truth. He has a narrow, immature reality, which reduces his scope for action. He ends up going round in ever-decreasing circles trying to deny the time loop. He tries to make the best of it yet gradually his resistance weakens. Depression eventually replaces his denial and anger. He becomes disillusioned and bored with being stuck in time once the novelty of his situation wears off.

Another key moment occurs when he realizes that he cannot win Rita. Manipulation no longer works. Up to this point he had a purpose: to win her. The goal of seducing her gave him a purpose and a plan for his days. When he fails to reach his goal, all purpose and meaning disappear. He has run out of steam, out of ideas, and out of hope. Once he accepts that he cannot win Rita, everything starts to unravel.

It has all been a game up to now. Now the game turns into a nightmare, symbolized by the image of the enormous clock slowly moving to six a.m., illustrating the enormous weight and inevitability of time. Phil walks more slowly, and looks disheveled.

He is just going through the motions. He learns all the answers to a quiz show and says them aloud to the astonished guests. But the difference is that he no longer enjoys his cleverness. All the spark and energy have left him. He faces the terrifying prospect of being trapped in time and space for eternity. At his lowest point, Phil proclaims his desolation to Rita: "You want a prediction about the weather; you're asking the wrong Phil. I'll give you a winter prediction. It's gonna be cold . . . it's gonna be gray . . . and it's gonna last you for the rest of your life."

He tries to take his own life, many times. Not even death can release him from the time loop. Phil has to accept that there is no escape, and in doing so the magic emerges.

Emerging on the Other Side

For while he still believes he can escape the time loop, he is unable to accept his predicament. It is only when all his resistance ends that he is able to move on and change. Paradoxically, it is only when he finally accepts that he cannot escape from Punxsutawney that he begins to make the progress that eventually leads to freedom.

Phil has to struggle through his own anguish and fear to

come out the other side to a place of acceptance. According to Buddhist thought, it is only when we cannot stand the never-ending cycle of misery anymore that we awaken. This echoes Phil's experience as he exhausts every possible alternative. Effectively, Phil is left with no choice but to accept the reality of his imprisonment in time.

He stops ruminating and accepts that nothing, or nobody, is going to rescue him. Phil does not have a teacher, as in the Buddhist tradition. It is all down to him. He is ready to take responsibility, though he still has to learn one more vital lesson of acceptance.

After his many failed suicide attempts, Phil realizes that he is immortal and believes he is a god. He displays his supernatural foresight to Rita as he accurately predicts a precise sequence of events and conversations in the café. Yet his new powers cannot save the old man. He has to accept that he is not a god, that life is imperfect, and that sickness and death are part of human existence. He cannot stop death. At last, Phil sees life f as it is, not through the distorted filter of his personal reality.

Acceptance Is Magical

Acceptance is magical because being honest with oneself is a major step to bringing about change. In *Groundhog Day*, the magic really begins when Phil's acceptance enables his old reality to die. A new one emerges that connects him to the world and to other people. Previously, Phil's old self was limited to self-absorption, which placed a boundary between him and other people. He could not get beyond his self-serving thoughts and behaviors until his reality collapsed.

The old Phil dies, since there is no point or meaning to his existence. If he had not been trapped in the time loop, he might well have gone far with his old reality—on to greater wealth, success, and power. He would also, most probably, have continued to be bitter, unfulfilled, and lacking in the intimacy of an authentic, loving relationship.

Phil's reality on entering Punxsutawney may be adequate for life as a TV weatherman. It is entirely inadequate for his imprisonment in the time loop. The real magic of paying attention to the repetitions and accepting his predicament is to expose the limits and weaknesses of his old reality and hasten its collapse.

Stripped of his TV persona, Phil has to stare into the abyss. He has to confront his emptiness in a world where his skills, earnings, and achievements have little or no value. Like many people who lose their jobs or retire, he has to find out who he is without the structure and meaning of a career.

Lessons Learned from Acceptance

Phil's shift from resisting to accepting his predicament can teach us some important lessons. Acknowledging the truth is challenging, because we do not like to accept that there is a problem and that it might be our responsibility—the result of our personal reality. We particularly don't like to accept that we might have to give up something we value.

We don't like to accept facts that conflict with our cherished beliefs, because it means questioning and confronting our reality which, as I described earlier, causes our minds a great deal of distress. I have a friend who has persevered for years in an unhappy, hopeless relationship. She clings desperately to the possibility that her partner will change, when all the evidence shows he won't. She cannot accept that she has made a mistake, and that nothing will improve until she faces the truth and walks away.

She would rather stay entranced by the Groundhog Day Effect than face reality. She would prefer to thrash around, trying harder and harder to persuade her partner to be the person she wants and needs, than challenge her old, repetitive thoughts and behaviors.

Our realities are designed to protect us from this truth. We don't want to think about problems, about illness, about death—so we busy ourselves with distractions. We try to fight reality, even though experience has shown us that we can never win. The longer we delay acceptance the harder it becomes. We hate getting older, losing our strength and energy. An obsession with youth and a denial of our vulnerability fuel our fear.

If you are in conflict with reality, you risk being frustrated and unhappy. If you spend your days wishing the past was different or that people would conform to your expectations, you are setting yourself up for permanent feelings of failure.

Not accepting reality can be very alluring. I have met people who continue to write novels believing they will be the next Stephen King, although publishers have turned down their previous fifty "masterpieces." They are stuck in their own fantasies and maybe a dose of reality would be unbearable. Unattainable dreams are fine for a while. The problem arises when the fantasy directs and dominates your life. What else could you be doing with your time? What is the impact on your relationships? How long will the fantasy work?

Not accepting reality disconnects you from other people and experiences. I know of many people who spend their lives fighting reality, unable to accept the truth. They will always believe that life is unfair or that the odds are stacked against them. They create a story about how unlucky they have been, seeing themselves as victims. They are always searching for something or hoping that luck will start running their way, and that people will start acting the way they want.

Ultimately, delusion fails because the world does not conform to how you think it should be. The world is as it is. If you spend all your days wishing that things could be different, you are prone to worry and anxiety.

When you are lost in anxious thoughts, you suffer from what psychologists call "rumination." Sonja Lyubomirsky, a leading researcher in this field, has shown that people who engage in excessive self-reflection tend to dwell on negative thoughts and worries, and that this rumination decreases their sense of well-being.[2]

A better strategy is to accept what you can and cannot change. You can change your personal reality but you cannot change reality itself, like the past or how other people think and act. When you accept what you cannot change you release your energy and abilities to focus on what you can change.

Acceptance starts to reconnect you with the real world. When you accept reality you see the world as it is, not through the distorted filter of your reality. The act of accepting yourself, your past, other people, and the world is extraordinarily powerful. Indeed, this is the first step for many effective change programs such as Alcoholics Anonymous[3] and Accceptance and Commitment Therapy.[4]

Even if we figure out what to accept and not to accept, making changes is still hard. We often prefer to resist the truth than accept it. When faced with trauma, we tend to react with fight or flight, acting as though we do not have any other choices. We run out of ideas and solutions. Recognizing the "box" we perceive ourselves to be in is tough enough; getting out of it is even tougher. Phil has to reach the depths of despair, and his old self has to die, before he gets out of his.

You might need your old self to "die" too. Until your personal reality collapses, everything you do will be limited by its structure and worldview. Once the collapse takes place you have nothing left, and from that emptiness emerges genuine transformation. Maybe we have to follow Phil through the "dark night of the soul."[5]

Phil only changes when he has no other alternative, revealing a fascinating irony of the human condition. We are very poor at changing until we are forced to, and then we are extraordinarily adaptive and creative. We always have the ability to change, yet only demonstrate it when we are forced to.

Maybe we also need to reach a point of no return, where the pain of continuing as we are is so much greater than the pain of changing. There comes a moment of truth

God grant me the serenity to accept the things I cannot change; courage to change the things I can; and wisdom to know the difference.

REINHOLD NIEBUHR

when the smoker knows, before she puts the cigarette in her mouth, that she is going to cough, and shorten her life. Acceptance is also triggered by a sense of urgency, like being faced with a life-threatening illness.

Accepting that change is hard is important, as is accepting that the struggle itself is the key to success. We tend to fall in love with the idea of change, but then flounder when we realize what is involved. Even the simplest change, like keeping to a New Year's resolution to go to the gym, becomes a huge burden. Yet research suggests that people who face adversity are often happier and more fulfilled.[6] It seems that you cannot just skip all the unpleasant "stuff" and get to the end. Great stories are stories of struggle.

"Now I Get It!"

If you can stay with the collapse of your personal reality and accept that it will not destroy you, you will become stronger. There is a period of confusion and uncertainty, a transition between the "old you" and the "new you." Part of you desperately wants to revert to the perceived safety of your old reality.

> *Desperation is the raw material of drastic change. Only those who can leave behind everything they have ever believed in can hope to escape.*
>
> WILLIAM S. BURROUGHS

You want to avoid the struggle, hang on to our old self, and find someone or something to divert or rescue you. You want to find the answer somewhere else. You hope that a guru or a perfect romantic partner will rescue you. Or maybe you should hang on for that big lottery win, or find solace in alcohol or drugs.

Whenever you look for something or someone else to rescue you, you become more stuck. Society offers false hope of rescue, and it rarely arrives. Once you accept that fame, wealth, power, looks, or status will not make you happy you are liberated to find a more secure and rewarding path.

Ironically, you learn more when you admit and accept

your ignorance. You recognize how little you know and how you have been held back by your "certainties." How often do you think you have "got it," that you have found the answer, only to find that it is not what you thought it was? When you open your mind and accept your ignorance you experience the real world, not a closed, narrow interpretation of it.

Have you ever said to yourself, "Now I get it!" Maybe you have read an uplifting book or listened to an inspiring speaker. When I get excited about a new idea, I think, "Now I get it!" and then I have to tell everyone about it. Everything

The truth that many people never understand, until it is too late, is that the more you try to avoid suffering the more you suffer because smaller and more insignificant things begin to torture you in proportion to your fear of being hurt.

THOMAS MERTON

is fine until I get the next big idea. I am not convinced we ever get to a point of certainty or enlightenment. I remember the description of fulfillment by the great British poet Philip Larkin:

> *. . . stumbling up the breathless stair*
> *To burst into fulfillment's desolate attic.* [7]

We hope there is a perfect end-state ahead, and we are all trying to make sense of the world and searching for a guiding structure. So when we discover a new idea that seems to answer one problem, we often use it as the solution to all our problems. The structure is very comforting and often provides stability and certainty when we most need it.

The classic case is someone in therapy who benefits from a particular insight or technique, and then applies it to everything they do and everybody they know. Everyone they meet is suddenly "co-dependent" or "recovering from their birth trauma." We get out of one box and climb into another.

More dangerous still are people who are convinced they have "got it" and insist that everyone else should too. How many of the world's problems are caused by people who regard anyone who has not got it as inferior or even evil? Ideological and religious fanaticism breed terrorism and war.

When we think we have got it we risk closing up and freezing ourselves in time. We stop learning and paying attention and try to replace our own reality with someone else's beliefs. When we believe that we have found the perfect way to live, and start living by a set of fixed rules, we gain some comfort in abandoning our personal search for meaning and adopting a set of ready-made solutions. We crave structure when there really isn't any. We prefer delusion to the truth.

Delusion and Truth

The deeper questions are, How do we know the difference between delusion and truth? How do we know what to accept? We have to accept certain things in life, such as stopping at a red light or paying taxes, but do we have to accept what our teachers, preachers, and politicians tell us?

When considering what to accept or not accept, ask yourself questions such as "Can I do anything about this?" or "What is my real intention behind accepting or not?" Are you deceiving yourself in order to maintain your old reality? For example, if you have trouble accepting that you are not going to be promoted at work, then examine your patterns of self-esteem and pride. Are you trapping yourself with self-deception?

No man is happy without a delusion of some kind. Delusions are as necessary to our happiness as realities.

CHRISTIAN NESTELL BOVEE

Similarly, managers at organizations need to accept the truth. Organizations have their own realities, and sometimes they need to be shattered for a turnaround to take place. In the 1980s, I leased IBM computer systems when IBM was the dominant technology business in the world. The accepted wisdom was that "you never get fired for buying IBM."

A decade later, IBM lost its way and suffered crippling losses of billions of dollars. In 1993, Lou Gerstner took over as CEO and led the transformation of "Big Blue" with massive changes to the leadership, culture, and organization. Corporate renewal was only possible with a new organizational reality. The old IBM, the computer hardware vendor, had to die for the new one, the technology solutions and services provider, to be born.

Ignorance Is Bliss

Sometimes we have to accept the predicament we are in, and make the necessary changes. Other times we just have to accept that we don't have the answers. I accept that I don't know and, indeed, can never know all the answers. After all, what do any of us really know? The universe is a mystery, and we should embrace this. We do not understand human consciousness and we do not understand how the universe works at a subatomic level. Quantum mechanics has exploded our view of science; it seems the more we learn the less we know.[8]

Acceptance that we don't have the answers also helps to clarify what is possible and what is important. It puts the onus on us to find meaning, to create our own personal reality and not take someone else's.

This is a harder way. It is tough to change our attitudes and choose what we want to believe in. It is far easier to adopt another's reality. Yet this voyage of discovery is magical, as you break free from your conditioning and choose how you want to live.

You can create a personal reality based on non-acceptance, of trying to change the world. Or you can create a personal reality based on acceptance, and making the best of what you have. This does not mean that you give up on your goals or stop searching for new activities and experiences. What it means is that you focus your efforts on what you can change: your attitudes, your skills, and your behaviors — not those of others.

I have always been disappointed by motivational speakers who claim that we can do anything and be anyone we want in life. I once asked one of them if I could win Wimbledon next year. As soon as he claimed it was possible, which would be quite something for a forty-year-old intermediate club player, I said that my friend also wanted to win Wimbledon next year too. This presented more of a problem.

You don't need to believe in ludicrous fantasies to improve the quality of your life. You cannot do anything and everything you want. Everyone has different talents. Accepting what those talents are, and are not, will help you. Ambitions and dreams are important, but we can't all be Steven Spielberg, Oprah Winfrey, or Roger Federer. Indeed, more professional career and training programs are focusing far more on identifying your core strengths, and building on them, rather than trying to be good at everything.[9]

Accepting your strengths and limitations can be a revelation. Once you quiet the voices in your head telling you what you can and cannot do, you gain far more clarity and self-awareness. It is so liberating to feel that you don't have to prove anything to your parents, to your friends, or to society. You can discern what is right for you and distinguish this from all your conditioned beliefs.

You will have to face facts, however hard that might be. Once you do this, your personal reality is in harmony with the real world, and you are balanced and at peace. This happens when your personal reality is based on accepting what is and having no desire for it to be otherwise.

> *Life is an immobile, locked,*
> *Three-handed struggle between*
> *Your wants, the world's for you, and worse*
> *The unbeatable slow machine*
> *That brings what you'll get.*
>
> —Philip Larkin,
> "The Life with a Hole in It"[10]

In this state of mind, you start to accept yourself and others. Judgment ends, acceptance begins. So does forgiveness, for forgiving people who have wronged you in the past releases a great deal of energy and allows you to move on.[11]

A Time for Everything

Perhaps even more important than accepting other people is accepting the nature of the human condition. This, in fact, was the turning point for Phil. When Phil accepts that the old man's time has come, he acknowledges the exis-

tence of suffering and death—that there is a time for everything.

To everything there is a season,
a time for every purpose under the sun.
A time to be born and a time to die;
a time to plant and a time to pluck up that which is planted;
a time to kill and a time to heal . . .
a time to weep and a time to laugh;
a time to mourn and a time to dance . . .
a time to embrace and a time to refrain from embracing;
a time to lose and a time to seek;
a time to rend and a time to sew;
a time to keep silent and a time to speak;
a time to love and a time to hate;
a time for war and a time for peace.

—Ecclesiastes 3:1–8

There is a time for everything. Co-screenwriter Danny
Rubin regularly asks, What time is it? Is it time for weep-
ing or laughing? Is it time to rend or sew? Maybe there is a
natural order to things that largely remains hidden. There
is "a time to be born and a time to die." Phil shifts through
the full spectrum of experiences, both good and bad. He
progresses through a series of stages that might seem
unnecessary or painful at the time, yet are essential to his
development.

He cannot experience the joy of love until he has experienced the sadness of rejection. He cannot feel hope until he has felt despair. He cannot find meaning until he has lost hope. When you believe there is a time for everything, you will feel calmer and worry less about the inevitable ups and downs you will face. There is a natural cycle to life.

This also means accepting the inevitability of our own death. In the West we are obsessed with antiaging and longevity, terrified of confronting our own mortality. This is unfortunate, because the thought of death reveals the truth about our reality. It clarifies who and what is important, and encourages authenticity. People who suffer near-death experiences often make dramatic changes in their lives.[12]

Phil not only contemplates death, he embraces it and finds new life by trying to kill himself many times. He endures great suffering before finding happiness and fulfillment. Few of us would want to go through times of despair, yet we rarely have the foresight or perspective to recognize their significance.

When we accept that there is a time for everything, we shift to a different level of consciousness, which helps us to gain perspective into the mystery of life. We cannot always judge whether a given event is good or bad at the time it happens. Sometimes we need perspective.

We might be stuck in a loop; perhaps we will always be stuck in one loop or another. What matters more is that we can go with the rhythms of life. When we want to, we can "go with the flow" and find pleasure in a lousy day. We can also observe and learn from our shadow side. When you feel angry, try accepting the anger instead of fighting it. Notice what happens as you observe yourself getting angry. Don't judge it, just feel it.

Other times, we know when it is time for change. Phil knew it was time when he stopped getting pleasure from exploiting the townspeople, particularly when Rita got progressively angrier with him. Have you noticed that your strategies are providing diminishing returns, and that you are not getting even the short-term satisfaction or gratification?

We cannot change anything until we accept it. Condemnation does not liberate, it oppresses.

CARL JUNG

The pleasure of buying a new car might only last a few days, or even hours. The latest travel destination looks the same as every other one, and eventually you find you've lost all interest in checking into another hotel. Symptoms that it is time to change also include ennui, a sense of being trapped, and the feeling that there must be a better way.

How much time have you spent on worry and regret, and where has it gotten you? Once you release the worry, the regret, and the anger—and accept life as it is, not as how you wish it would be—you are able to move forward. You have started to escape from the Groundhog Day Effect that has kept you trapped.

When we end our resistance to reality, we stop fighting

life and learn to dance with it instead. The core of our personal reality is altered and new hope and possibilities begin to flow. Now that you have accepted reality and your inability to control it—now that you have accepted your limitation and the limitations of others—you can start to accept yourself and take responsibility for your life. This is magical.

In *Groundhog Day*, when Phil Connors learns to accept his limitations, he abandons his old self and constructs a new personal reality. Faced with a situation he cannot control, forced to accept that he is not God, Phil no longer tries to change his circumstances or manipulate them to his advantage. He begins to accept his life and face reality head on. This triggers a magical change. Phil accepts that he cannot beat the time loop, so he makes the best of the situation by discovering the magic of creativity.

CHAPTER SIX

The Magic of Creativity

We never know where the inspiration for our creative endeavors will come from. At one point in *Groundhog Day*, after Phil has taken Rita into his confidence and told her about being stuck in time, they are in his room talking. As Phil teaches Rita to flick cards into a hat, she asks him, "Is this what you do with eternity?" This plants a powerful thought in Phil's mind. Then she suggests that eternity could be a blessing in disguise: "I don't know, Phil. Maybe it's not a curse. It just depends on how you look at it."

Rita might not be his muse, but she has planted the seed of change in Phil. He realizes that he can change and create a new life. He acknowledges the possibility that his life isn't a pointless hell. Now he has hope, and hope is magical. Phil gives us the hope that we can change, that life could be so much better

Phil learns to re-create his own life. He had always has been creative to some extent, and he progresses through different stages of creativity during his time in Punxsutawney. Understanding these different stages will help us create a new personal reality, which is the catalyst for our transformation.

Manipulative Creativity

As soon as he realizes that he is stuck in the time loop, Phil starts to reflect on the content of his days and discovers he can choose to do whatever he wants. Moreover, his creative potential is unlimited because there are no consequences to his actions. He does not need to work, he has no responsibility. He can do anything he wants in the knowledge that he will wake up the next morning with a blank slate.

Nothing will have changed in the town, and nobody will remember what happened, apart from him. Phil changes by learning to be more creative in how he uses this one day. Ultimately, he creates the perfect day and a personal reality that needs nothing more than what he had in Punxsutawney on February 2.

Phil learns to be resourceful as he experiments with his repetitive day. Stuck in a freezing small town in the middle of winter, he has to find inventive ways of spending his time. He decides to make the best of things, if only to play pranks and have a lot of self-indulgent fun.

He gathers information about people and then uses it to

manipulate them. He learns the personal details of a lady called Nancy, and the next day pretends he knows her from school and proceeds to seduce her. Since she does not remember giving him the information the previous day, he can take advantage of her.

Similarly, he closely studies an armored truck arriving at the local bank, then plans and executes a perfectly timed robbery. Since he knows the exact movements of the guards, he can use a window of opportunity to steal the money from the truck.

Phil is very playful. He dresses up as Clint Eastwood in a spaghetti western to go to a movie. He drives on a railway with some local drunks and deliberately gets arrested. His creativity is childish and narcissistic.

By experimenting, Phil learns which strategies work and which do not. He learns to be more resourceful and creative in his use of time. Eventually, he is able to create a magical day with careful planning. When Phil and Rita are walking in the snow, she says to him, "Thank you for a very nice day. It's the kind of day that could never be planned." To which Phil replies "Well, it can be planned but it takes a lot of work."

Being resourceful is demanding; it requires great determination and resilience. When Phil realizes he is trapped, his world literally collapses. He is forced to deal with being alone, without anyone who can understand him. The local doctor and psychotherapist are of no use. He must fall back on his own resources with no support structure.

Now that his *outer* structure has been removed, he has to dig deep and find an *inner* structure. He has to move beyond his personality and find something stronger and more resilient. What has worked for Phil before, in his career in Pittsburgh, is now an obstacle to his development and even his survival in Punxsutawney.

The old strategies are failing. Even promiscuity has become monotonous and routine. He has reached the limits of a personal reality based on selfishness and pleasure seeking. He is stuck in a mundane day and, like other "entitled" people who generally get what they want, he starts to fixate on the one thing he can't have—Rita.

Phil uses all his resourcefulness to seduce Rita. Night after night, he learns every possible detail about her life. He spends his days learning French poetry to impress her. He knows her preferred drink, her favorite toast, and her hopes and aspirations.

He then uses this knowledge in conversation to try to build rapport with her. He pretends to have the same interests and values, and every night gets closer to her. It looks like he will trick her into his bed, when suddenly his strategy stops working. She intuitively knows there is something wrong and accuses him of obtaining personal information from her friends.

Magical Creativity

It is only when Phil starts to see the time loop as a blessing rather than a curse that he discovers a magical form of creativity. This is another defining moment of the movie. Phil's creativity and resourcefulness are no longer working; he has run out of steam. Finally, he stops using his creativity to amuse himself and manipulate others. Instead, he uses the same capacity to enrich his life as well as the lives of others. He entertains and delights himself and the townspeople with piano playing and ice sculptures. He stops wasting his time flicking cards and memorizing all the answers on TV quiz shows. Instead, he takes up reading. Reading expands his world and his possibilities. He had probably never read a book unless it was assigned, or unless he thought it would help him get rich or attract women. Now he takes pleasure from reading for its own sake.

He decides to learn the piano. He finds a teacher and embarks on a course of lessons that take him from beginner to virtuoso. After all, what better way to spend eternity than to use the time to learn to play an instrument? Even if Punxsutawney is stuck in February 2, Phil can still measure progress by his musical ability. This would be a return on his investment in time. With each day the same as the last, hundreds of hours of practice on the piano or time spent making ice sculptures will bear tremendous fruit.

Excellence in the arts requires a long-term commitment, one that Phil would never have made before. He might have thought about playing the piano and admired great pianists, but there is little chance he would have found or made the time to learn. By taking a long-term view, his perception of time changes and, more significantly, what he can do with time.

As his skills improve, Phil sets up a positive loop. The better he becomes at the piano and ice sculpting, the more pleasure he finds, and the more dedicated he becomes. The magic of creativity takes him from a downward spiral of self-pity and isolation to an upward spiral of accomplishment.

This is a great way to spend his day. Absorbed in his new passions, time passes quickly. It does not matter so much that he is trapped in eternity, because he appreciates the quality of each moment. Artistic pursuits give him meaning and purpose.

The more Phil spends his time on creative pursuits, the less time he spends dwelling on his predicament. He is also creating a new personal reality for himself. He might not be able to change his external world, but he can change his perspective.

Phil changes the way he sees other people. One of my favorite moments in *Groundhog Day* is when Phil recites the following lines of poetry to inspire his fellow hotel guest the same guest he had previously ignored and later pushed up against a wall in anger: "Winter slumbering in the open air wears on his smiling face a dream of spring.

When I watch this scene I think of the hundreds of hotel guests and staff I have avoided making eye contact with, or engaging in conversation with over the years. Always in a rush to meals or meetings, I shun all human contact. Yet once in a while I chat with someone in the elevator or at the next table in a restaurant and feel better.

Phil develops a new response to create a wonderfully uplifting moment of real warmth. Now that his old self has died, he is re-creating Phil Connors as he invents new experiences, new feelings, and new connections. He is moving beyond self-absorption to absorption in creative activities. He has shifted from agonizing over the best way of ending his life to entertaining a hall of people with his musicianship.

A Creative State of Mind

Phil discovers two types of creativity that facilitate his progress. The first is the *skill* of creativity through pursuits such as music and art. The second is the *state* of creativity, a mind-set that enables him to reinvent himself and build a new personal reality. The way he benefits from both offers us some fascinating insights that help us find the same magic in our own lives.

There is room for both creative and uncreative pursuits. Sometimes all we want to do is watch TV or sit around doing nothing. The risk is that we suffer from not having any creative interests or hobbies at all. If shopping is our only leisure activity, and all we do is consume rather than create, we are denying ourselves a great source of pleasure.

I have had the good fortune to run a successful business, teach at Oxford, and travel the world. Without question, I am happiest when I am writing. Even in business it is the development of the idea that most engages me. My father was at his happiest when he was painting, and most people I know would rather be engaged in artistic activities if they had the chance.

The point is to find the time. I know writers who get up at four in the morning to write before work. I bet there is a good chance you would like to be able to play the piano like Phil does in the concert. What would it be like to play Rachmaninoff rather than download the MP3?

Time sometimes flies like a bird, sometimes crawls like a snail; but a man is happiest when he does not even notice whether it passes swiftly or slowly.

IVAN TURGENEV

When we are playing the piano, writing, or painting we are enjoying what psychologist Mihaly Csikszentmihalyi calls the state of "flow."[1] When you are in a state of flow you are completely absorbed, losing track of time and self-consciousness.

Performing the task is rewarding in itself, and you enjoy a feeling of accomplishment. You don't need to be Eric Clapton to enjoy playing the guitar or Tom Hanks to enjoy amateur dramatics. Being the best or being competitive isn't the point. The point is the process of creativity and the benefits it provides to your mind and your spirit.

When you are in the flow you are focusing on performing a satisfying task rather than dwelling on your own needs and concerns. You create a new, positive loop in which you lose your sense of self and time and are fully present in the moment. Phil is in the flow on his last February 2 in Punxsutawney. Like a talented artist he creates a masterpiece using of the material of his twenty-four hours.

Creativity is the supreme human quality. Our ability to create new thoughts, new beliefs, and new behaviors is our most powerful magic. It gives us the power to choose how we want to think and how we want to live.

Every block of stone has a statue inside it and it is the task of the sculptor to discover it.

MICHELANGELO

(ATTRIBUTED)

Above all, it gives us the power to *consciously* create a new personal reality and break free of the *unconscious* Groundhog Day Effect caused by our old one. We have an infinite number of potential futures before us; we are only restricted by lack of imagination. When we broaden our vision, it is like rising above a dense, impenetrable forest and seeing the way out. We recognize how our reality has trapped us, and that we can free ourselves too.

When we are trapped in the Groundhog Day Effect, we are lost in the forest with limited paths before us. When we transcend our reality we can see that many paths lead out of the forest. With different ways of interpreting and experiencing the world, we can take the path that is right for us today, not the one that was right for us as children. We can choose to do the right thing rather than the easy thing.

Inner Creativity

A creative state of mind also offers us the intriguing possibility that we do not need to be creative in the traditional sense of the word. What if life was perfect already and all you needed to do was change our interpretation and perspective? What if you were to direct your ingenuity inward rather than outward? The potential implications of this are intriguing.

Indeed, who is more creative—the person who spends their life engaged in "outer" creativity striving to be a great painter or playwright, or the person who spends their life engaged in "inner" creativity striving to be happy and peaceful? Moreover, who is more likely to achieve their goal? The answer probably lies in combining both forms of creativity, as Phil does when he recognizes that he has to be inventive in his actions and his thinking to make the best of his time.

Phil's creative state of mind enables him to be very resourceful and very experimental. He learns how to make the best of the cards he has been dealt. How about you? How resourceful are you? Do you see your life and each day as an experiment in how to live?

When you think of your life as an experiment, you open up many new possibilities. You can generate new ideas, new thoughts, and new behaviors. With an open and flexible mind-set, you let the magic emerge rather than stifling it as we are conditioned to do.

Such a mind-set also increases your number of choices.

You move beyond your fight-or-flight responses to people and events. Everyone has to choose how to make the best of their resources. A person with a serious disability can be much happier than the richest celebrity simply because she has a better strategy—one that is proactive, positive, and creative. There are extraordinary stories of resourceful people who triumphed under the most adverse conditions. Think of Helen Keller who was born deaf and blind, yet went on to read, write, and become an inspiration to millions.[2]

How well do you handle adversity? How resilient are you? I am convinced that we are able to learn more from failure than from success. The question is how well we bounce back from failure. Phil has to bounce back every day. He has to try hundreds of different strategies before he makes progress. Similarly, a creative person learns to make the best of her resources, whatever challenge she encounters.

Resourcefulness

Inner creativity leads to resourcefulness, and the Groundhog Day time loop is the ultimate scenario for learning this vital skill. The loop forces Phil to be resourceful. He has to continually find creative strategies to deal with his deepest fears and break free of his conditioning. This is genuine education, because what seemed to be the worst events of his life lead to the biggest breakthroughs in his growth.

Life is his teacher, and he has to struggle with archetypal forces such as fear and fate to make progress. He is playing an extraordinary, magical game. At first, he does not know the rules or the outcome of the game. He never knows what force is keeping him in the time loop. Over time, he begins to understand the rules better. The game lasts twenty-four hours, and every morning at six a.m. the game resumes with all the pieces back in their original position. Only Phil's knowledge of the game has changed.

His challenge is to use the resources of the game as creatively as possible and to find a way out of the game itself. The resources he has at his disposal are the town, its people, and the day. He has to develop a strategy to win the game without a manual to help him. Knowing he only has twenty-four hours, he becomes expert at cramming everything into his day, and this intense cramming teaches him how to get the most out of life

Phil has to overcome many obstacles; he is sidetracked by detours, false starts, and distractions along the way. Most of his responses and strategies fail, and it takes him hundreds, maybe thousands of days of repetition to make any progress. Even when he thinks he is making progress, he is not. For scores of days he thinks he is winning Rita's affections when, in fact, he is losing her.

How will you act with your resources today? Will you make the best of your day? Like Phil, you can become more resourceful when you change your attitude toward life, the world around you, and time itself. One suggestion is to choose carefully the metaphors you use to make sense of the world. Be conscious of your self-talk. You could wake up and see the day ahead as something to get through or as a blank canvas on which you can express yourself creatively.

Creative Time

Using time wisely does not mean being more efficient or getting more things done in the same amount of time. Multitasking in itself can lead to an obsession with saving time. The number of things we do is less important than what we do and how we do it.

Half our life is spent trying to find something to do with the time we have rushed through life trying to save.

WILL ROGERS

When people reach the end of their life they often regret the time they wasted on the wrong activities. Impending death forces them to reflect on their past. Phil's predicament is similar, since the trauma of being trapped forces him to think about his past and his present.

Every day gives him a chance to revisit his past and alter his future. He is able to go back to every encounter, every incident, and improve it. He becomes an expert at crafting his life. When you wake up tomorrow, think of the day ahead as a blank canvas on which you can paint anything you want. As you learn to craft your life, you will discover the ability to create your own masterpiece.

Tomorrow might be very similar to today. You might be

unable to change the place or the people, but you are able to change your attitudes, thoughts, emotions, and actions. You have more control over the outcome of your day than you might realize. You decide if today is something to endure or a unique opportunity to be imaginative. Is today a dreaded routine or a chance to open up new possibilities?

The day is of infinite length for him who knows how to appreciate and use it.

GOETHE

Creative Action

I believe that creativity is the best strategy to break free of the Groundhog Day Effect. It makes you more flexible and more responsive. I have found that the most successful and the most fulfilled people tend to have the widest range of strategies, tools, perspectives, theories, and skills. They focus on changing themselves rather than trying to change other people. They are more resourceful and able to find creative solutions to any challenge they face

Creativity begins when you simply make small adjustments to your daily routine. Changing your behavior can change your reality in subtle ways, and broaden your horizons. So join the Latin dance class, watch a French movie, listen to a CD of Japanese folk music.

You do not have to wait to be creative. You can start the process whenever you want and wherever you are. You simply design a strategy for approaching each day and, most important, take action.

The key is to create new loops and new habits. This also takes courage. Phil takes risks because he has no fear of death. He knows he will wake up every morning, whatever happens. He learns to spend his days developing new skills and becomes far happier by doing so.

Genuine creativity means that you take a risk. You try something original and you overcome your fears. You build positive new loops absorbed in the flow of stimulating

> *Creativity can solve almost any problem. The creative act, the defeat of habit by originality, overcomes everything.*
>
> ⌒
>
> GEORGE LOIS

activities, and thereby change your personal reality. Now you have the resources and the capability to create your own magical day.

CHAPTER SEVEN

The Magic of Love

Many people love *Groundhog Day* as a great comedy, and many love it as a great love story. Phil's developing love for Rita is the catalyst for his transformation, and we can see how love does indeed conquer all.

In the previous chapter, we saw how Rita ignites the flame of hope in Phil. With her help, he no longer envisions a life with the limitations of his old reality. He builds a new life, focusing his efforts on creative pursuits. A new, broader vision is emerging: one receptive to new experiences and activities.

Phil is learning to love life first, before he can truly love another—or even himself. For a while, he leads a solitary existence, absorbed in reading, music, and art. These are rewarding, though he risks losing himself in constant activity without learning to embrace other people. Maybe he believes that there is little point in forming relationships because they cannot be sustained and developed. After all, nobody will remember him, or what he says or does, the next day. There would be no point to friendship in his "one day" lifetime.

At this stage, he may still be looking for something in return. He can see the benefit of his investment in the piano; he cannot imagine any benefit from a similar investment in connecting with others. He does not care how well anyone knows or understands him. He can never enjoy a long-term, mature relationship.

What at first seems exciting becomes tragic. All he wants initially is a one-night stand, and he knows that he can get Nancy into bed by the end of the day. The problem is that long-term relationships are impossible. For a while he was living the fantasy of many single men: sex without any responsibility. Yet the fantasy loses its allure and Phil realizes that he is condemned to a series of sexual encounters without any emotional engagement or meaning.

With no hope of reciprocity, Phil has to concentrate on what he can do for others rather than what they can do for him. He discovers the magic of unconditional love—love that brings great joy; love that neither wants nor expects anything in return.

Once more, the unique nature of his predicament creates a set of conditions for his learning. The final lesson in the class of Punxsutawney is on the subject of love and meaning. The repetitive day forces him to see and experience the benefits of connecting to others, helping them, and feeling unconditional love.

Love for Love's Sake

When Phil's old personal reality collapses, so do the boundaries he has built between himself and everyone and everything else. He is not isolated and disconnected from the world anymore. The lives of others are as important as his, since they are all part of the same indivisible reality. He no longer judges or manipulates other people because they are connected to him. He and they are "all one."

Phil is fully present and engaged in life for the first time. Like a prisoner emerging from a dark cell, he appreciates the joy of living as his senses open up again and he savors each glorious moment of his new reality.

While reading in the restaurant, Phil hears some classical music playing on the radio. He has probably heard it a thousand times before, albeit in the background. On this particular February 2, he listens to it and is touched by the musical muse. His senses are beginning to come alive like a plant's first shoots in spring.

At last he is waking up! Everything is starting to click. His speech and actions flow naturally from his newfound love. He does what he loves and loves what he does. He takes pride in his work and in playing a positive role in people's lives. He has moved from the periphery to the heart of the community.

By discovering the magic of love Phil also finds his authentic self, which remained hidden under all his old prejudices, selfishness, and remoteness. Previously, Phil was inauthentic. All his words and actions were carefully scripted in a desperate attempt to project a false image, particularly while trying to seduce Rita.

His deceit and self-centeredness were a comforting diversion from the dread of being trapped in the time loop. By seeking fun and exploiting others he had less time to worry about anyone or anything else. He simply moved from one unhealthy loop of repetitive patterns to another. The problem was that he soon got stuck again.

His pattern of self-indulgent behavior was unsustainable. Once the initial euphoria of enthusiasm evaporated, Phil was left with very little but vanity and pride. His achievement and status were devalued by the absence of love, connection, and authentic feelings.

As Phil starts loving, he opens up emotionally. When he helps the old man, he sees him as a fellow human being, not an irritating distraction on his way to the Groundhog Day ceremony. When Phil feeds and cares for him it feels right, and when he cannot save him he is genuinely upset. The death of the old man is the defining moment that leads Phil to release his emotions and expose his vulnerability. He cannot hide from pain and suffering anymore.

As Phil gets in touch with his emotions, he strengthens his connection to other people and to life itself. By learning to love himself he is able to love others. He discovers a whole new emotional landscape to explore, delighting in the intense sensual nature of his new life. Since his mind is full of love, he has no room for selfish, negative thoughts. Feeling the irresistible need to go out and help people, he has no choice other than to act compassionately.

This is a very different Phil. When he first arrived in town, he was solely concerned with his own needs; now he is solely concerned with the needs of others. His days are devoted to chivalry, laughter, and music. He is affectionate not distant, optimistic not cynical, humorous not sarcastic, and relaxed not tense.

The New Phil

Phil's final day in the time loop is probably the best of his life. It is full of passion, joy, and love. He is a different person from when he first arrived in town. He is not richer, nor has he acquired more qualifications. What he has is a new reality. He has transformed his thoughts, attitudes, feelings, and behavior. He has broken free of his old patterns.

He even appears and sounds different. He looks much happier, and his physical appearance and his voice have changed. He is relaxed and comfortable with himself, and with other people. He has replaced sarcasm with empathy, and bitterness with cordiality. When the movie ends, you can feel his extraordinary joy during that last magical day in Punxsutawney.

Phil's psychological age has increased, even if his physical age has not. Playful and empathic, he is reminiscent of the Laughing Buddha. He has a spring in his step, his body language is open, expressing his joie de vivre. Life is no longer a struggle. It is a magical dance.

Phil could have continued forever learning new skills and becoming the most accomplished person in history. The risk was that his creativity might have simply become another distraction, another way of avoiding the lack of meaning and joy in his life. He could have anything he wanted, except for the love of others.

Come out of the circle of time and into the circle of love.

RUMI

Phil finds meaning by using his creativity with loving intention. He applies his unique power of foresight to create magic in other people's lives, and by so doing makes his own life more magical too.

Instead of planning bank robberies or seductions, he now plans how to help the boy falling out of the tree, the old ladies in a car who need their tire changed, and Buster, the Groundhog Day official who is choking on food in a restaurant.

Phil discovers that serving others is far more fulfilling than serving his self-gratification. This is a magical discovery. He does not need to spend years in a monastery, or be trained by a guru. He learns by doing good, and moves from hating the town to loving it.

He begins by casting his shadow over Punxsutawney and ends by illuminating it. At first, Phil knows nothing about the local people and only the barest details about his colleagues from the TV station. He is only interested in Rita because she looks after what he calls "the talent" and she can find him a better hotel. As he begins to pay attention and learns to be creative with his day, he awakens. And then the townspeople come alive for him too.

This is magical. People who were previously "hicks," or even "morons," become important to Phil. They are no longer obstacles to his plans or objects to be exploited. Attending to their needs becomes the center of his everyday activities. They magically come alive as he learns to love ordinary life, with all its foibles, in small-town America.

Reaching Out

Phil gets to know the stories of everyone he meets, and appreciates that they are decent people with feelings, hopes, and dreams just like him. Many of them are trapped in their own Groundhog Day, just like he is. There is Bill the waiter who has not told anyone he is gay, and Gus who hates his life and wishes he had stayed in the navy. As he gets to know everyone, he stops judging them and starts caring for them.

He learns that kindness is superior to cleverness, and that his life is no longer a curse. It is a blessing, and it does not matter if every day is the same. He has changed.

For a long time, the world of Punxsutawney revolved around Phil, and he had good reason to feel self-important. Only he knew what was going to happen, and only he could learn from the previous day. He does not have to be powerful and controlling any more. He does not need to play any more tricks. He is acting naturally and not trying to prove anything or impress anyone.

Maybe Phil had to spend hundreds of days repeating his acts of kindness until he was appreciated. It does not matter because what

I would rather feel compassion than know the meaning of it.

THOMAS AQUINAS

counts most is Phil's authenticity. He is being honest and not trying to project an image anymore. He acts with genuine compassion because he wants to, not because it is the "right" thing to do.

Phil genuinely enjoys helping others. He performs good deeds for their own sake, not for rewards or kudos. He does not want to be admired as a philanthropist or to boost his public image. After all, with no tomorrow, nobody will remember what he does anyway.

He also helps people in the right spirit. He helps people with enthusiasm, grace, and humor. Their concerns are now his concerns. When Phil catches the boy who falls from the tree, the boy runs off without thanking him. Yet, day after day, Phil continues to save him irrespective of whether he is thanked or not

Phil does not change through good intentions; he changes

by engaging with the world and through his relationships with others. As he serves others he also reinforces his compassion. He starts to see the results of his actions, and that there are consequences to his behavior. He knows that if he does not help others they will suffer: the boy will hurt himself when he falls out of the tree and Buster will choke to death in the restaurant.

Phil does not insult people with sarcasm and drive them away as before. He inspires others with his good humor and vision of life. He boosts their self-esteem and draws them to him like a magnet. He even changes his opinion of the Groundhog Day ritual from derision to admiration.

This change of heart is reflected in the opening statements he makes in his telecast. He goes from "This is one of those times where television really fails to capture the true excitement of a large squirrel predicting the weather" to "When Chekhov saw the long winter, he saw a winter bleak and dark and bereft of hope. Yet we know that winter is just another step in the cycle of life. But standing here among the people of Punxsutawney and basking in the warmth of their hearths and hearts, I couldn't imagine a better fate than a long and lustrous winter."

Phil and Rita

Phil loves the town, its people, and the ceremony. Above all, he loves Rita. His relationship with her reveals the full extent of his extraordinary transformation.

At first, Phil tries to seduce Rita through ingenuity and deceit. In his mind she is the object of his game: prey to be hunted, not a person with her own needs. He learns every detail he can about her life in order to impress her. He adapts his own personality to match hers, promoting a false self in the hope of winning her over. He employs the same flirting and seduction techniques that are promoted in many books and magazines. This is about power not intimacy; it is lust not love. He gets so far with his act, until the moment when he tries to get Rita into his bed on their first date. She is having none of it.

Phil tells Rita that he loves her, but she is scornful and says to him, "You don't even know me." She then realizes that she has been manipulated: "This whole day has just been one long setup." Now she is angry and tells him bluntly, "I could never love someone like you. You only love yourself." His response to this is very revealing: "That's not true. I don't even like myself." Phil has been using his creativity to project an inflated image to win Rita's affection, because he does not believe she would care for the real Phil.

Rita exposes Phil's insecurity and insincerity. She is the unmovable rock that his manipulations and lies cannot shift. She is the benchmark against which he must measure any progress he is capable of. She has always been authentic and loving. She is not pretending or playing games. It is Phil who has to get real and grow up.

Once Phil recognizes that he cannot seduce Rita, he

becomes desperate and gives up any further attempts. Accepting that he cannot win her through his seduction techniques, he starts to pay attention to her as a human being, not merely as the object of his desire. He recognizes her true qualities, telling her,

"You're a sucker for French poetry and rhinestones . . . You're very generous . . . You're kind to strangers and children . . . And when you stand in the snow, you look like an angel."

Phil is only ready for Rita when he becomes a loving person like her. He is no longer playing a role nor does he have a hidden agenda. He stops *pretending* to be the man Rita might fall in love with and starts *being* that man. It is only when Phil acts authentically, discarding his projected image, that he makes the breakthrough with Rita.

Taking a "Rain Check"

He cannot fake compassion and love. Rita only falls in love with Phil when he is genuinely compassionate and loving. She knows this intuitively, just as she knew earlier that he was a fake. By loving people, Phil becomes lovable. Even at the end, when Rita wants to spend time with him, he puts the needs of others first. He tells her, "Can I have a rain check? I've got some errands to run."

He is not acting to impress Rita. She does not even see his "errands" as he saves the boy and the official, and helps the old ladies with their car. Knowing that they will have accidents at specific times, he places their needs above spending time with Rita.

He is a loving person, and is not faking love to win her affection. Indeed, she does the chasing at the end, when she bids for him at the auction. Now their relationship is built on a solid foundation of mutual affection and honesty.

Phil has found an even more profound love than romantic love. He is feeling love and compassion toward humanity. This is what the Greeks called *agape* in contrast to *eros*, which is the passionate love for another person. Phil loves his life. He loves himself, and is loved by Rita.

Phil had already fallen in love much earlier, but after the series of debacles when she first rejects him, he decides not to pursue her. He does not believe she could ever love him. Now she does the pursuing because she is attracted to his compassion and sincerity. Her love is the key for Phil to open the door to tomorrow.

When he tells Rita that "no matter what happens tomorrow, or for the rest of my life, I'm happy now," he is released and able to move on to the next day, February 3. Phil has fully embraced the present moment, other people, and the world around him. His old self has dissolved. He has completed the last stage in the journey to a magical day.

Phil is creating a new reality founded on love, not selfishness. He is also aware that he is connected to other people's realities and is part of a much greater existence. For the first time, he truly appreciates the majesty of life.

By experiencing immortality, Phil gains a new appreciation of his own mortality. He leaves the time loop and returns
to normal time, facing the certainty of eventual death with
new insights and the resolve to make the best of every day.

Once he is mortal again, he knows with all his heart
what is most important in his life, and builds his future on
the timeless qualities of love. He discovers the magic of
ordinary life through the magic of his extraordinary experience. Back in "real time" he is able to appreciate the simple pleasure of building a relationship day by day.

Liberated from the time loop, he has a new appreciation
of how he wants to live. He plans to exchange a TV career
in the big city, with all its trappings, for the peace and calm
of small-town life. He wants to trade the exciting fast pace
for a slower rhythm, and swap status and fame for love.

Letting go of what he thought he wanted, he finds what
he really wanted and needed all the time. It might have
taken him many years of repetition and practice, but he
gets there in the end. He no longer needs the admiration of
others or the material comforts of a high-paying job. Punxsutawney, the town he tried to escape from, has everything
he ever needed. In the last scene in the movie, he even suggests to Rita that they live there, or at least "rent to start".

Lessons in Love

Phil has completed his amazing journey and escaped the
time loop. So how do we find the same happiness and ful-

fillment in our lives? How can we discover the magic of love and find authenticity, connection, and meaning?

I am not sure if we can emulate Phil intentionally. It is very difficult, and risky, to engineer the collapse of our reality. Our natural inclination in times of crisis is to dig in our heels and fall back on the familiar and trusted coping mechanisms of our personal reality. Phil could only do this for a limited time because the repetition of the day forced him to see that his old reality was failing and he had to change.

Unlike Phil, we can generally run away and revert to our old selves. Perhaps the key is to recognize those moments when our world is falling apart and allow ourselves to experience it, knowing that we can build something much stronger.

We can also weaken our reality more gently as a prelude to change. By observing our patterns or loops and challenging them with new patterns of thought and behavior, we starve our old reality of the oxygen it needs to survive. If you are someone who craves control, try letting go and experience how it feels, moment to moment. Having let go once, it is a lot easier to do it again.

A friend of mine is a very successful entrepreneur who struggled to let go for years. He was a control freak who supervised every aspect of his business and family life. Everything was planned and managed, nothing instinctive and spontaneous. Always tense and guarded, he was stuck in a loop that stopped him from feeling authentic love.

It took a serious heart attack to wake him up and smash the personal reality that had trapped him in his cycle of control. Forced to take six months off from work, he reevaluated his life. He learned to delegate in his business and genuinely enjoy his family for the first time. Moreover, his business improved and, as the magic of Groundhog Day reveals, what seemed to be a disaster led to a triumph. Fortunately, we do not need to wait another day for fate to intervene in this way

Acceptance

Try using the magic of Groundhog Day. Accept being stuck, and pay attention to the repetitions in your life. Then develop creative new responses and, most important of all, act lovingly and authentically.

Phil makes his final breakthrough when he allows love to enter his life, and so can you. You might feel that love is confined to romance or family. The Groundhog Day love is much bigger than this. It is about loving yourself, loving life, loving other people, and loving the world.

It is the unconditional love of Christianity, or the compassion of Buddhism. It is the sensation of awakening and experiencing an overflowing joy. Above all, it is a feeling, not a thought or an abstract concept.

Major personal change is usually accompanied by catharsis. It is not a neat, controlled quick fix. When you let go of your old self there is a tremendous release of old emotions. This often happens in therapy or during times of tremendous stress. Sometimes our emotions are stored physically and can be released by deep massage.

A first step to letting go of your old self is to simply to allow yourself to fully acknowledge your emotions. Often when we sense a powerful emotion, such as fear or anger, we want to control or avoid it. This only serves to give that emotion more power than ever and bolsters the Groundhog Day Effect.

We also avoid painful emotions by escaping into projects like starting a business or a house renovation, or into addictions like drink, drugs, shopping, or sex. The antidote is to be aware of your emotions and break free of your trance. Instead of running around in circles looking for something or someone to "complete" you, give yourself all the time you need to experience and accept your feelings. It is the holding back of feelings that keeps us trapped, and the release that liberates us.

You know quite well, deep within you, that there is only a single magic, a single power, a single salvation . . . and that is called loving. Well, then, love your suffering. Do not resist it, do not flee from it. It is your aversion that hurts, nothing else.

HERMANN HESSE

We are loving when we feel love. Some people find that connecting and serving others encourages this. Buddhists believe that once we feel our own suffering, and become aware of the nature of suffering, we want to alleviate the suffering of others. If you have ever witnessed suffering firsthand, such as being with a dying parent or friend, you know that it changes you.

Helping Others

When Phil helps others it is because he wants to, not because he feels an abstract sense of duty. Indeed, he has to do good, since this practical expression of love is a natural extension of his new self. There is no shortcut to this overwhelming need to love and serve others. Perhaps the best we can do is to start performing good deeds and notice what happens.

So if you want to emulate Phil, try an experiment. Make a list of three good deeds you want to do tomorrow, and then do them. Phone a relative you have not spoken to for years; offer your time to a local group of volunteers; visit the new neighbor on your street. Do not think too hard about it. Just perform three good acts every day for a month and record how you feel.

Practice makes perfect. Look at what Phil achieves in a day when he redirects his energy from serving himself to serving others. This is the magic of love. By altering the core of his reality from selfishness to love, he goes from being a cynical outsider to the most popular guy in town.

You appreciate the extent of Phil's transition when you observe the full spectrum of his responses to the insurance salesman, Ned Ryerson. Starting with denial, Phil moves

through avoidance, contempt, anger, violence, over familiarity, and — finally — genuine friendliness.

Phil only had the people of Punxsutawney to engage
with. You have the world. Yet you can learn from Phil by
starting in your own community. Start small and go deeper
into the world around you. Then you will see the results of
your actions.

When you love you transcend your personal reality.
You redirect your energy to focusing on other people's
realities. As you do this, your own reality loses much of its
power, and many of the worn-out, negative thoughts,
beliefs, and desires that keep you unhappy disappear. Your
old expectations, rules, and conditions seem to melt away,
and a deep sense of fulfillment emerges in their place.

You replace your old loop of self-absorption with a new,
reinforcing loop of positive action and feedback. As you do
more good, you strengthen the feeling and achieve more
for yourself — and for other people too. Now repetition
works in your favor.

Spiritual leaders and philosophers have been telling us
about the magic of love for many centuries. What is so
interesting is that modern scientific research seems to support their claims. There is hard evidence for the magic of
love.[1]

You also enhance your physical and psychological well-
being when you help others. Studies show that people who
volunteer seem to be happier. This is a magical equation.
You help yourself when you help others.[2]

My particular interest is the environment, and I have
worked on conservation campaigns where I learned firsthand the great feeling of working with good people for a
worthy cause. When we come together voluntarily in the

*If thou do ill,
the joy fades, not the
pains. If well, the
pain doth fade,
the joy remains.*

GEORGE HERBERT

pursuit of a cause greater than ourselves, something magical happens. It is the perfect remedy to the
cutthroat competitiveness of modern life.

Whatever you decide, do it in
the right spirit and without expectation. It does not matter what
other people do or don't do, or

what they say or don't say. Everyone is at a different stage
in their lives. Phil's stage is unique in Punxsutawney. He
has the opportunity to develop at a much faster rate than
the townspeople, because he is able to observe and learn
from his actions every day. He helps people and does not
judge or lecture them.

Humility

Phil offers us a lesson in humility. Sometimes when we do
good deeds, or discover what we believe are deep spiritual
truths, we tend to feel morally superior. This is not authentic compassion. Our so-called good deeds are serving our
personal reality's yearning for approval and achievement.
We quickly forget what we used to be like, and conve-

niently overlook our faults. The good deeds become yet another way of boosting our egos.

I have frequently helped others when my real motivation was to earn approval and reciprocity. When I think this way I am really doing good to help myself, not to help others. It might be better to perform good deeds than not, but it is not true compassion. Authentic compassion will help others and help you too, but only if you have no expectations or strings attached to it.

Compassion

Sometimes it is easier to be authentic with strangers than with our families. Nowhere is the Groundhog Day Effect more powerful than at home. We lock in to patterns of behavior and responses that block empathy and understanding. When was the last time you really listened without judgment to your spouse, your partner, or your children?

If you feel stuck in a particular relationship, it might be because you are stuck in a damaging pattern of communication or non-communication. Try communicating with compassion. Look into the eyes of your spouse or child and consider, in the words of Maya Angelou, how they would want you to make them feel. Then you stop focusing on what you want, and give them what they want. Soon you grasp that the two are the same.

So look around you. Who in your family or among your friends and colleagues needs your attention? Who can you engage with? Who can you communicate with in a way that breaks through old dysfunctional patterns?

When you connect to others you are also more likely to find meaning in your life. Phil finds meaning and purpose by connecting with others. We are social animals and need connection. We might *want* to control other people, but we *need* to connect to them.

> *I've learned that people will forget what you said, people will forget what you did, but people will never forget how you made them feel.*
>
> MAYA ANGELOU

Meaning

A life without meaning is unfulfilling. A tough, repetitive existence is bad enough. Meaningless repetition is far worse. During the Victorian era, British prisoners were put on treadmills to drive machinery. Some of the prisoners found solace in doing useful work, so the authorities disconnected the treadmill from the machinery, to make it a meaningless activity. This proved to be a worse punishment. Have you ever felt as though you were walking on a treadmill without purpose?

Perhaps the most powerful example of the importance of meaning is found in Victor Frankl's book *Man's Search for Meaning*.[3] Frankl was a psychiatrist who survived World War II as a prisoner in Auschwitz and other death camps. He showed that even in the worst circumstances imaginable, we have control over our inner life. As long as we find meaning and hope, we can survive. He believed that our main concern as humans consists "in fulfilling a meaning and in actualizing values, rather than in the mere gratification and satisfaction of drives and instincts."

Making Connections

When meaning is removed we face despair, as Phil did when he attempted suicide. He ultimately finds meaning through his connection to other people. It is doubtful whether Phil would have changed so radically if he had been marooned on a desert island for the same period of time. In those circumstances he would have learned to appreciate the importance of connection only through its absence.

How connected are you? How much do you know about the people at work? How many of your neighbors do you talk to at length? When you meet people, do you evaluate them straight away in terms of their value to you. Are they attractive, well dressed, wealthy? Do you think, "What can they do for me?"

Everyone judges others. We live in a world dominated by networking for personal gain. When we enter a room we scan people, looking for signs of their potential value to us. Everyone we meet has to help us in some way; they have to contribute to our personal and professional goals. We don't have time for friendship anymore, unless it pro-

vides a specific benefit like promoting our career or helping with our fitness plans. How often do you just "hang
out" with people like you used to do at college?

Phil has the time to make friends, yet it takes him a very
long time to get around to it. Maybe it is only through the
constant repetition of contact that he develops any form of
relationship. Imagine if you knew everyone on your street,
all the intimate details of their lives, like Phil does. Would
you stop stereotyping or judging them, and develop friendships
instead?

I love mankind;
it's people
I can't stand.

CHARLES M. SCHULTZ

So if you want to bring the
magic of *Groundhog Day* into your
life, make acquaintance with your
neighbors, and be active in your
community. When you pay attention, your local streets stop
being anonymous thoroughfares on your commute; they
come alive as places full of life. There are extraordinary people and stories in your midst. There are hidden lives waiting
to be brought into the open. There are people on the periphery of your vision waiting to be brought to the center.

When you open your eyes, you open your heart. You
realize that your neighbors are just like you, and they are
probably feeling as disconnected as you are. Try listening
to others. Stop thinking about what you need to be doing
next, or what else you could be doing, and simply be present with that person in the moment.

When you are aware and authentic, people are no
longer a projection of your personal reality. You realize

that they are separate human beings with feelings, thoughts, and needs similar to yours. This can lead to a magical shift in consciousness that benefits both you and them. Like Phil, you discover the joy of intimacy. Phil only had twenty-four hours to build relationships before people would forget him. You have the benefit of normal time and people who remember you.

Once Phil connects to people, he devotes his days to helping them feel good. What if you were to do the same? Think for a moment of all the daily transactions you have with people by phone, email, or face to face. Now imagine what would happen if you saw each one as an opportunity to improve their mood or brighten their day. You don't have to make big, sweeping gestures that might seem insincere or pretentious. Just add a simple courtesy or acknowledgment. Just soften your tone of voice or offer a welcoming smile.

Engaging with people is very hard. Overcoming shyness and caution, we open our hearts up to others and make ourselves vulnerable. We have all had the experience of trying to make friends and being rebuked or exploited. Jean-Paul Sartre wrote: "Hell is other people." Ever feel that way?

Expand Your Circle

Nowadays, we prefer to stay safe by mixing with people like ourselves. We tend to form our social networks on shared interests, beliefs, and education. These networks are also described as our "social capital," and we prefer what is known as "bonding social capital" to bridging social capital." Bonding refers to associating with people like ourselves, such as when we join a golf club; bridging refers to associating with a far more diverse group of people from different racial, religious, and educational backgrounds.[4]

Phil enjoys bridging social capital. He does not spend time with lots of media types, aside from Rita. He meets people from all walks of life and learns to see the value in all of them. Through Phil we can appreciate the pleasure of genuine community, friendship, and relaxed conversation. One of the reasons so many people love *Groundhog Day* is that we are nostalgic for the security and familiarity of small-town life, where we know our neighbor and have time for a chat. We want to find our own Punxsutawney. We want to come home.

Phil finds his home in Punxsutawney. He becomes noticeably happier as he bonds with people, and we want to feel the same. Moreover, an increasing amount of research demonstrates a strong link between our well-being and our relationships. Our number of friends is a far stronger contributor to our happiness than our number of possessions.[5] Yet according to the *American Sociological Review*, the average American man has only two friends.[6]

Authenticity

We crave friendship and, above all, we crave intimacy. Phil found love with Rita when he replaced fake intimacy with authentic intimacy. If you have to spend all your energy proving your worth to someone else, exaggerating your qualities and promoting your achievements, you risk building a relationship founded on illusion. By creating the illusion that you are perfect, you are selling yourself as a product.

We find real love by being loving first. Love is the magic that breaks down the boundaries between Phil and the townspeople, and between him and Rita. When he feels love, everything changes. He is no longer a spectator; he is a participant in life. People like him as Phil Connors the man, not Phil the TV personality.

When he finds love, he finds meaning and he acts with compassion. Moreover, the more he helps others, the more loving he becomes. He not only escapes the time loop, he also creates a new loop based on the timeless qualities of love, authenticity, and meaning. He is connected to other people, the world and, most of all, himself.

There is no certainty that we will find the love that Phil does. What I do believe is that if we transcend our self-centered realities, we increase our chances of finding love. Then if we cultivate a new reality based on love, we increase our chances even more. For, after Phil has been trapped for thousands of day; after he has tried every possible tool and technique to cope; the only strategy that works is love. He learns what we all learn and what we have always known, that love is the one true magic.

CHAPTER EIGHT

A Magical Life

I f you had only one day to live, what would you do with it?

How do we explain Phil's transformation? How do the magical qualities of repetition, awareness, paying attention, creativity, and love work together? In this chapter we'll explore Phil's transformation in depth and review a wide range of religious, philosophical and psychological interpretations. Underlying each interpretation is the shift in Phil's personal reality. I will suggest some ideas for re-creating this in our own lives.

To recap, Phil experiences exactly the same day in the same place with the same people thousands of times. The day never changes. His attitude and feelings toward it do. He experiences the full range of emotions about this one day. It is a frustrating day and a fun day, a depressing day and a hopeful day, a dull day and an exciting day. This day makes him contemptuous of the town's inhabitants and also makes him feel compassion for those same people. It even makes him want to kill himself. And it enables him to find love.

In the words of Charles Dickens, Groundhog Day has been the "best of times and the worst of times." It has been both the most terrible day of Phil's life and the most amazing day of his life. So what happened? How could this one day contain everything, from despair and attempted suicide all the way to great joy and hope?

The day remains the same. Phil's experience of it changes. This raises some interesting questions. How much of Phil's change was intentional and how much was accidental? If it was intentional, can we apply the principles he learned in order to change to our own lives?

Your Magical Day

Phil has lived his magical day. So how about you? What is your magical day? What would you be doing, who would you be with, and how would you be feeling? For some people their magical day is their wedding day, for some the birth of a child, and for others it is a simple day spent in the countryside or on the beach. Despite their differences, magical days include common ingredients. They normally involve spending time with loved ones, enjoying fun and laughter, and experiencing peace of mind and delight.

Phil's transformation may have taken many years of hard work, but it does not occur randomly. He may have been through every possible emotion and opinion about his time loop, yet he does manage to create this magical day. And so can you. Think of what it would be like to live in a never-ending February 2. What would you do? Now think of the next week as the same, the next month, the next year. The challenge is not so different from real life is it?

Interpretations of the Movie

Groundhog Day, like all great stories, is timeless and universal. It might be set in twentieth-century America, but it could be take place anywhere at any time. It deals with so many enduring themes, including redemption, midlife crisis, and the heroic journey undertaken in epic works like *Ulysses* or *Siddhartha*.[1]

Millions long for immortality who don't know what to do with themselves on a rainy Sunday afternoon.

SUSAN ERTZ,
ANGER IN THE SKY

Phil has to deal with eternal endeavors such as conquering fear, fighting inner demons, and finding true love. Yet, simultaneously, Phil's predicament symbolizes the more commonplace contradictions and tensions of the modern Western lifestyle: the contrast between big city and small town life, the challenge of finding meaning in a consumer society, and the emptiness of celebrity.

The Existentialist View

There are a number of potential philosophical interpretations of the *Groundhog Day*. The most obvious one is Friedrich Nietzsche's concept of "eternal recurrence,"[2] which maintains that events will recur again and again for eternity. He wondered how we would live if we knew that we were going to live our same lives again.

As one of the first existentialists, Nietzsche proposed that the greatest challenge facing human beings was the search for meaning. Existentialists, including Jean Paul Sartre and Albert Camus, believed that the purpose of life was to overcome fear and isolation and discover our own meaning and philosophy for living, like Phil has to in the movie. Essentially, it is down to us as individuals to choose how to live our lives.[3]

According to this interpretation, Phil faces and resolves an existential crisis. He confronts his own mortality and discovers an authentic life, inferring that there is a state of "being true to ourselves." Yet maybe when Phil was acting like a jerk he was also being true to himself, and this was just another type of "being."

The Aristotelian View

The implication seems to be that authenticity means virtue, and that Phil creates a "good life" in the Aristotelian sense. He seeks to develop his character by pursuing excellence in the arts and culture, and by using his time wisely to perform good deeds. According to Aristotle's philosophy, Phil becomes a good person by performing good deeds. Happiness is achieved through a lifetime of such virtuous living, not pleasure seeking. Aristotle called this concept *eudaimonia*. [4]

The Solipsistic View

A completely different philosophical take on Phil's experience is provided by the theory of solipsism, the belief that only you exist and everyone and everything else is an illusion. It would be easy for Phil to feel solipsistic, because he is the only person in his world with an awareness of being in the time loop and the knowledge to use it to his advantage. Everyone else could seem like a passive character in a mysterious play.

So in this context life becomes like a game, and Phil develops strategies for optimizing his resources and boundaries. Moreover, we often do the same too. Even if we do not believe that we are the only person alive, we can still act as though we were. When we focus exclusively on our own needs, we fall prey to narcissism, a form of solipsism.[5]

Whatever way you look at it, *Groundhog Day* raises profound philosophical questions. How would you act if you could predict the future? How would you change if you lived for thousands of years? And, most profound of all, how would you deal with immortality?

The Judaic-Christian View

Such questions lead us to the religious interpretations of the movie. For example, is *Groundhog Day* a Christian parable about salvation? I am not sure, but I do see strong parallels between *Groundhog Day* and Ecclesiastes. In this book of the Old Testament the author, whom scholars believe may be the son of King David, describes the folly of his life of overachievement. He has achieved everything he ever wanted, only to find emptiness thereafter. "Vanity of vanities; all is vanity!" Ecclesiastes 1.2. Ultimately, he only finds happiness in love and living simply, just as Phil does.

Hindu and Buddhist Perspectives

A Hindu perspective of the movie would stress the significance of reincarnation. Each day is like a lifetime as Phil is "reborn" every morning and "dies" each evening. Phil's purpose is to learn profound lessons through this condensed daily cycle of death and rebirth, until he sees through *maya* and reaches *nirvana*.[6]

In 2003, *Groundhog Day* was featured in a movie series at the New York Museum of Modern Art called The Hidden God: Film and Faith. At this event Jews, Christians, Hindus, and Buddhists all claimed that the movie represented their particular beliefs.[7] Perhaps the most popular theory is the Buddhist perspective that Phil transcends *dukkha*[8] and attains enlightenment, or *satori*.[9] In doing so, he becomes a bodhisattva devoted to helping people escape the suffering of the cycle of birth, death, and rebirth.

Karma, the principle of cause and effect central to Buddhist and Hindu thought, resonates throughout the movie. At first, Phil believes there are no consequences to his actions, and he indulges in his fantasies claiming, "I am not going to play by their rules any longer." He does what he wants, and commits crimes with no care for the consequences, because there are none.

It takes a long time until he finally grasps that, although there is no tomorrow, his actions still have consequences. *Karma* is real, and he can observe the effects of his behavior on other people. When he is bored, he wakes up bored and has a bad day. When he becomes compassionate, he wakes up with purpose and can see the consequences of his good deeds during the day he performs them.

While in the time loop, Phil lives in this world but is not of this world. Phil is human but lives in a timeless mystery. He does not know who or what is causing the time loop, just as we do not understand the mysteries of the universe All we can do is make the best of what we do know.

In Conclusion

The exact meaning of Phil's transformation is also a mystery. Does Phil extend the boundaries of self, transcend his self, or cast off his separate, individual identity altogether? You can choose to think that Phil has moved to a higher level of consciousness, that he is reborn, or even that he is the same old Phil, and his enlightenment is only temporary.

Groundhog Day's co-screenwriter Danny Rubin and I have discussed the possibility that rather than creating a new self, Phil discovers his true, authentic self. Danny even suggests that creativity and discovery might be the same process. In some ways, Phil discovers the splendor of his true, loving self, much like Michelangelo "discovered" a beautiful statue in a block of marble. Maybe Phil finds magic in both losing and discovering himself.

I do not think there is a definitive interpretation, and there does not need to be. If you choose to see it as a religious story, that is fine. Like all great art, the movie is open to many different interpretations. I am more interested in identifying a universal process for creating a magical day, irrespective of one's beliefs.

A Universal Model of Transformation

Does an explanation exist for what happened to Phil that is independent of any specific religious interpretation? Can we identify universal processes that are replicable and as close to a systematic theory as possible? I believe we can. In fact, the more scientific the explanation, the easier it is to define the concepts, understand the processes, and recommend useful practices. Then we can get closer to emulating Phil's transformation.

We can, indeed, create conditions that will initiate and

encourage our own transformation. These conditions derive from a number of compelling and well-established psychological models. Perhaps the best-known and most relevant is Abraham Maslow's concept of "self-actualization." When you are self-actualized, you have realized your full potential as a human being. This concept seems to explain Phil's development fairly accurately.

A self-actualized person is someone who is psychologically healthy. According to Maslow, such a person displays the following qualities:

- They are "open to experience."
- They have an "accurate perception of reality."
- They are "attracted to the unknown."
- They enjoy a "freshness of appreciation."
- They are spontaneous and creative.
- They are accepting and stable under pressure.
- They prefer to focus on problems outside of themselves rather than be introspective.
- * They are autonomous; they feel genuine empathy to other people and the wider world.[10]

This lists of traits corresponds strongly with Phil's character development. By the end of the movie he is accepting. He pays attention by being open to experience, developing a freshness of appreciation while maintaining an accurate perception of reality. He is creative and spontaneous, acting autonomously and experimenting with the unknown, He connects with other people and develops genuine empathy to others and the world.

Such an interpretation also parallels Jung's theory of "individuation"[11] and Eric Erikson's model of life-stage development. According to Erikson, Phil progresses successfully through the three adult stages of development: from "isolation" to "intimacy" in his relationships with others; from self-absorption to "generativity" a life full of creativity and purpose in the service of others; and from "despair" to "integrity" bringing all the strands of his life together to find meaning. In many ways, Phil matures from adolescence to adulthood.[12]

Sudden Change

More recently, William Miller and Janet C'de Baca wrote a book entitled *Quantum Change* that documents their investigation of case studies of sudden transformations or epiphanies. They propose that quantum change is a "vivid, surprising, benevolent, and enduring personal transformation." Even though Phil did not necessarily make a sudden change, the authors find common patterns among the different case studies. These patterns are quite similar to Phil Connors' experiences of in *Groundhog Day*. Quantum change includes a shift in priorities from wealth, achievement, attractiveness, and career to personal peace, growth, spirituality, and happiness.[13]

These case studies are supported by a large body of

contemporary research that is exploding the myth that achievement and wealth will make us happy. Certainly, money is transformative if you live in poverty; it will make a positive difference if you earn less than forty thousand dollars a year. Beyond that figure, however, extra wealth adds little to your sense of well-being.[14]

When we are under the spell of the Groundhog Day Effect, we uncritically accept certain cultural assumptions. One of the most important of these assumptions is that we will improve our lives through earning and consuming more. But evidence shows that when we get what we think we want, the feeling of pleasure is fleeting. We vastly overestimate the anticipated pleasure of our material goals.[15]

Moreover, when we focus on our gratification and short-term pleasures, we reduce the possibility of finding genuine happiness. This is confirmed by the increasing numbers of psychologists who are studying happiness, under the banner of "positive psychology."

The Study of Happiness

Positive psychology research is helping to identify the causes of happiness, and also contributing to the development of models and tools that will promote it. Its findings explain why Phil is so much happier at the end of the movie, and provide convincing evidence for the different types of magic I have introduced. Indeed, the evidence seems to confirm that we are each able to create our own magical day.

Positive psychology research findings suggest that the happiest people share these characteristics:

- They are optimistic.
- They enjoy meaning and purpose in their lives.
- They have more good friends than most of us.
- They are married.
- They are part of a community.
- They volunteer more than most of us.
- They have survived adversity.[16]

With the exception of being married, these characteristics describe Phil. During the movie, Phil becomes more optimistic, finds meaning and purpose, engages in the community of Punxsutawney, volunteers to help the townspeople, and definitely survives adversity. Overall, the results suggest that the keys to happiness are to move beyond self-absorption and make connections with people; and to find work that is both enjoyable and meaningful. Furthermore, Phil's new relationship with Rita should bolster his well-being, even if it does not immediately lead to marriage.

Personal Reality as the Key

If such a wide variety of interpretations are supported by the events in *Groundhog Day*, then doesn't that reveal that it can mean anything or nothing? Reassuringly, there are strong similarities among the different spiritual, philosophical, and psychological interpretations. I believe the common denominator is what happens when we change our personal reality.

Your personal reality is your map of the world, how you make sense of your experience. It is the primary cause of the Groundhog Day Effect and keeps you stuck in repetitive patterns. It is only when you change your reality that you break free, by addressing the causes, not the symptoms, of the effect.

If we take the spiritual interpretation, it may be that Phil's personal reality, or his individuality, has been completely dissolved, and he is experiencing the world directly in a state of higher consciousness or enlightenment. I am not sure that any human can experience the world directly, however enlightened he is. I do not believe we are capable of functioning without some level of filtering, and I prefer to conclude that Phil has fundamentally altered his personal reality.

In simple terms, Phil has converted an unhealthy personal reality to a healthy one. He has converted from a way of seeing the world that keeps him isolated, and for the most part unhappy, to one that connects him to the world and gives him joy. I do not believe he transcends his personal reality or becomes divine. His new reality is available to everyone.

We all have to interpret the world, and the question is whether one interpretation is superior to another. Phil progresses through multiple realities, yet I want to focus on the

difference between his reality when he first arrives in Punxsutawney and his reality when he finally escapes the loop.

Old Phil and New Phil

It is clear that Phil at the end of the time loop is very dis-
similar to Phil at the beginning. Let's use the names "Old
Phil" and "New Phil" to describe the difference. We could
say that Old Phil was trapped in an unhealthy reality and
that New Phil is energized by a healthy reality.

So how does Old Phil turn into New Phil? Does he
have to go through hundreds of intermediary realities, or is
it a straightforward transition? Obviously, he does not
deliberately follow a religious path or the sequential steps
of a therapeutic program. He never sets out intending to be
a better person.

Indeed, I doubt whether Old Phil would have liked the
new one very much. The changes happen painfully and
gradually. He learns from experience, by trial and error.
He tries and eliminates every alternative way of dealing
with his predicament until he finds the one that works. We
can learn from his trial-and-error method.

The first step is to differentiate between a healthy and
an unhealthy reality; then you are better able to evaluate
your own. You can start by checking how you feel most of
the time. What is your life like right now? How effective is
your worldview or your personality? Is it making you
happy or sad? Is it making you well or sick? To find the

answers, let's look at the four specific differences between the two types of reality in terms of our emotions, needs, beliefs, and behavior.

Repressed Emotions vs. Authentic Emotions

First, an unhealthy personal reality represses emotions or creates unhealthy or inauthentic emotions. At first, Phil is incapable of connection or love. His emotions are either shut down or dependent on his desire for approval and status. He feels impatient and angry that he is trapped in Punxsutawney and cannot get on with his career.

When we are inauthentic, we are dependent on our roles for meaning, and on others for our self-esteem. We continually project an image, based on our personal reality, which takes up much of our energy.

A healthy personal reality encourages authentic and positive emotions. Over the course of the movie, Phil develops positive emotions like hope, empathy, and compassion. He feels his own pain and the pain of others. He also feels genuine love. He opens up and experiences a catharsis as he releases the harmful emotions of his previous personality.

When we are authentic, we are aware of the present moment, our feelings, and our thoughts. We have abandoned our scripts, transcended our roles, and escaped the Groundhog Day Effect. Our self-esteem comes from within, and our actions are congruent with our values. Our emotional maturity enables us to develop genuine intimacy in our relationships.

Shielded from Reality vs. Facing Reality

Second, an unhealthy personal reality helps protect the psyche of a child. Its formation is motivated by unmet childhood needs like approval or security. Old Phil can only be happy if he is achieving and receiving approval. He is also driven by entitlement and gets upset if he does not get what he wants or feels he deserves. A healthy personal reality meets the needs of adult life, enabling us to deal with the problems and crises we all face.

The unhealthy "child" version might work for us as adults, when everything is going well and we have nothing to worry about, but it is poorly designed for handling challenges such as illness or aging. It crumbles in the face of such challenges. A healthy personal reality is resilient. It does not function only when everything is perfect or under control. Your happiness does not depend on circumstances and people outside your control.[17] Instead, it is motivated by genuine needs, like finding fulfillment and love. New Phil no longer needs fame and status; he needs meaning, connection, and intimacy.

Irrational Attitudes vs. Rational Attitudes

Third, an unhealthy personal reality consists of irrational and damaging attitudes that limit your happiness and thwart your development. Such attitudes include the belief that you must never be wrong, or that you are superior or entitled to success.[18] Old Phil's attitudes include the view that small towns are dull, that he is the talent the world revolves around, and that happiness means getting a better job.

A healthy personal reality consists of rational attitudes such as the belief that you can be happy irrespective of how successful you are or how you look. People with a healthy personal reality take responsibility for their own judgments and actions. New Phil develops healthier attitudes as he learns to value the small town, regards himself as part of the community, and recognizes that happiness is based on enjoying the moment and helping others.

Unhealthy Behaviors vs. Healthy Behaviors

An unhealthy personal reality generates unhealthy behaviors. These can include selfish, aggressive, or addictive behaviors. Old Phil acts without interest in anyone other than himself. He alienates other people and then tries to manipulate them for his personal gain. He seeks solace in binge eating and drinking, or in meaningless diversions like learning all the answers on TV quiz shows.

A healthy personal reality, on the other hand, generates healthy behaviors such as creativity, learning new skills, and serving others. New Phil lives in the moment, communicates with empathy, and has great fun helping others.

New Phil—In Summary

There is no doubt that New Phil is a completely reformed character. He is in a better mood, he looks and sounds different, and his behavior is remarkably improved. He has broken free of his old reality, discarding the dysfunctional patterns and habits of his old personality. He has a different set of values, a different perception of time, and different intentions. He has found a new zest for life, and the quality of his daily experience has risen dramatically. He has moved from being closed to being open, from resisting life to accepting it, from being selfish to being compassionate.

By changing his personal reality, he has changed his state of mind, and does indeed see the town, and life itself, through "new eyes." This is magical. What was previously unseen is now visible. What was boring is now exciting. The same people whom he once scorned, he now cares for. He has altered his consciousness without drugs, without a guru, and without divine intervention. Phil's transformation implies that we can, in Milton's words, "make a heaven of hell."

Phil finally escapes Groundhog Day when he learns to enjoy his life. Once he stops treating his time as a game and becomes more compassionate and authentic, he breaks free of the time loop. He has been forced to reflect on who he is without the normal supports of his life, outside and beyond his normal reality. Perhaps the healthy reality was trapped inside Phil all along, and, paradoxically, it was only by being physically trapped that he could liberate himself psychologically.

Phil escapes the Groundhog Day Effect. He discovers a clear, purposeful path forward and stops going around in circles, restlessly looking for ways to satisfy his ego. He is *internally* motivated by the pleasure of what he does, not *externally* craving rewards or others' praise.

Phil develops his own healthy reality, and we can do the same. He changes because the repetition of the same day forces him to pay attention to his life and the world around him. With his new awareness he accepts that his old reality has failed, and this hastens its collapse. By removing his fears, ambitions, and craving for approval, he releases a tremendous amount of energy, which clears the way for building a new reality based on love. This the final stage of his transformation and also liberates him from the time loop.

Old and New Phil—A Summary

What I find fascinating is that, while the time loop might be a supernatural phenomenon, Phil's development seems entirely natural and independent of time, place, or culture. I might identify more with Phil because he lives in 1990s America, yet I recognize something here that is a timeless, universal insight into the human condition.

Indeed, thousands of years of spiritual, philosophical, and psychological theories and practices seem to point to a similar conclusion, and *Groundhog Day* lays down a well-established path for us to go down.

I have created the following table to help demonstrate the scope of Phil's transformation. It identifies the main characteristics of Old Phil and New Phil. Sometimes it is difficult to notice change as it happens in our lives, and the

movie allows us to fully appreciate and measure the specific differences between Phil at the beginning and Phil at
the end.

Unhealthy Personal Reality	Healthy Personal Reality
Old Phil	New Phil
Unaware	Aware
Past and Future-focused	Present
Conditioned	Spontaneous
Unappreciative	Appreciative
Resisting	Accepting
Insecure	Resilient
Dependent	Independent
Rigid	Creative
Narrow Choice	Increased Choice
Selfish	Compassionate
Apathetic	Passionate
Stagnant	Fulfilled
Empty	Meaningful
Self-absorbed	Empathic
Isolated	Connected
Resentful	Loving

Some of Phil's characteristics remain the same—he is
always playful and funny. But most facets of Phil's personality are different. How about you? When you look at this
table, which column best describes your personality?

Which qualities do you want to change, and which qualities do you want to develop? Do you want to live like Old Phil or New Phil? If you answered "New Phil," then how do you get there?

The Way of Phil

It seems obvious that a healthy personal reality is the way forward. So why don't we just adopt one? The problem is that knowledge and intention on their own are insufficient. Our default reality restrains us, weakening our resolve. Furthermore, we often believe that we have moved into the second column when we are in still in the first. We might believe we are being empathic, when it is simply a means to boost our self-image.

We tend to deceive ourselves and fall for quick fixes. Remember that Phil has thousands of days to get it right through repetition, observation, and fine-tuning. He applies the same dedication to his life as he does to learning the piano. His last day in Punxsutawney is the culmination of years of practice.

You might need a lifetime too, yet it all starts with a single moment and ends with the accumulation of thousands of moments. Indeed, what matters most is the moment-to-moment decisions you make; the subtle shifts of direction that help to shift you from an unhealthy to a healthy reality.

Thoughts turn into actions and then into habits. Over time, these habits magically form a new personal reality.

The magic unfolds when you pay attention to the small details of life: the way you approach a task, the way you interpret someone's behavior, and the way you communicate. The magic unfolds when you accept the reality of your life and face the challenges that worry you. It unfolds when you create new choices as you respond to adversity, and discover a purpose that will encourage you to act with love and find meaning.

The new Phil Connors is not richer, better looking, more famous, or more qualified than the old one. He is happier and more fulfilled, though. So I find the contrast between the two Phils invaluable. I ask myself, What would Old Phil do here and what would New Phil do? It helps me readjust to be more like New Phil, especially as I am often stuck somewhere between the two.

I Am Phil and Phil Is I

I also find it useful to think of the Old and New Phils as two personalities competing for my attention. For much of my life I switched between the two, like a pendulum swinging between anger and acceptance, pessimism and optimism, and fear and courage. Both personalities were there all the time in my mind, and I flipped between them depending on my mood, energy level, and the weather.

Over many years, I habituated to the profound swings. Then I realized that I could promote the New Phil and suppress the Old Phil parts of me by taking charge of my moment-to-moment awareness. I could never completely eradicate the latter, but I could encourage and strengthen the former.

Now when I meet someone I don't particularly like, or am stuck in a pointless meeting, I am able to catch myself responding like Old Phil and immediately switch to being like New Phil. The more I do this at key moments, the more I am able to turn a bad day into a magical day.

I simply recall the contrast between Phil's first day in Punxsutawney and his last. I remember how much more he achieves in a day, how much happier and vibrant he is, how he connects with people, and the rewards of his efforts. Then I think through the following process of transferring the magic of the movie into my own life.

1. The day in the time loop is exactly the same.
2. Only Phil can change, and he can only change himself.
3. Phil changes his experience of this same day by changing his personal reality.
4. Phil turns February 2 from the worst day into the best day of his life.
5. Phil's transformation is based on proven tools and techniques that are available to me and you.
6. I can also turn this bad day into a magical day right now!

CHAPTER NINE

A Magical Career

W hen we change, the question becomes whether or not we will be able to bring these profound changes into the "real" world. A true test of any kind of fundamental change in attitude is whether or not that change can withstand the rigors of our daily life. In particular, once the euphoria starts to wear off, how well can we cope with the pressures of the workplace?

Do you revert back to the Old Phil when you go to the office? Do you cast a shadow over your team with your bad mood? Do you focus on everything that is wrong with your managers and how your clients do not appreciate you? Are you endlessly plotting how to advance your career at the expense of others. Or seizing every opportunity to raise your profile while putting your colleagues down? Do you feel that your job is a means to an end, and that you lack any genuine meaning or purpose in your work?

Or are you like the New Phil? Do you illuminate the office with your bright mood? Do you connect emotionally with your colleagues and clients, and focus on helping them get what they want? Have you found a vocation you are passionate about, one that gives you a deep feeling of authentic meaning and purpose? Have you attained a wonderful balance between your work and home life, and integrated your values and interests in both settings?

When I am working I ask myself, "What would the New Phil do?" Although I have learned, used ,and taught hundreds of tools and techniques for performance improvement and change management, I have found nothing more powerful than that simple question. When I ask myself this I immediately remember the movie and feel better. I switch instantly to a more positive mood, and choose to act how I think the transformed Phil would.

This technique is simple, fun, and easy to remember. Moreover, nowhere is the transformation from Old to New Phil more needed or more sought after than in the workplace. Faced with the threat of lay-offs, outsourcing, and hyperchange, many corporate employees are suffering from their own Groundhog Day Effect characterized by repetitive anxiety, fear, and insecurity. Stuck in the daily grind of mindless routine, employee engagement and morale is low; sickness and absenteeism high.[1]

Billions of dollars are spent, and often wasted, in countless organizational change programs throughout the world. For several years, I was president of a business called Quantum Leap Coaching, which worked with hundreds of executives and employees to bring about change. I taught similar techniques to many nonprofits and my students at Oxford.

For most people, work is not magical. I believe that we can learn a great deal from *Groundhog Day* about how to be more effective, develop invaluable habits, and attain a balance between success and happiness in our careers. In the following pages I will describe how we can emulate the New Phil to transform our performance and discover the magic in our work. We can replicate much of what Phil goes through and use the five types of magic to help to shift us from our old reality to a new one.

Paying Attention

When I give lectures I don't start by talking about business models or superior performance or market share. No, I begin by stating that the most important skill we need in business is "relaxed alertness." We should be calm and aware. When we pay attention to what is going on at work, we are able to recognize the true nature of our experience and the repetition that characterizes it. We can challenge and weaken the hold our personality has on us. We start to appreciate what we have rather than what we don't have, and this, in turn, weakens the compulsive patterns of our anxiety and restlessness.

When we pay attention, we slow down and focus on the present moment. We are better able to complete tasks rather than being fixated on the past or future.

We also pay close attention to our personal reality, because that frames everything we do. Until we break down our old reality and build a new one, nothing will change. With this in mind, I find it fascinating how managers are always trying to change everybody else, yet rarely address their own realities—the critical dimensions of all change. When we are mindful of how we think and how we act we are ready to change ourselves, and only then help others change.

Once we have done this we can attend to what is most important. We are able to prioritize and decide how we should best spend our time, rather than blindly following the routine or the incessant demands of responding to phone calls and emails.

We are able to catch ourselves immersed in the Groundhog Day Effect, and break free by consciously choosing where to place our attention. This self-discipline is the foundation of the most successful people I know. The ability to do what is necessary, however hard, rather than what is easy, is the hallmark of top entrepreneurs and CEOs.

Repetition

When we pay attention to the repetitive nature of our work we begin to see our habits. Sometimes these are obvious, like our tendency to get distracted while surfing on the Web. Other times they are more insidious, like our tendency to avoid confrontation or give up too easily in negotiations.

Repetition forces us to observe and understand our patterns, and evaluate what is or is not working. We see how the Groundhog Day Effect impacts our work, and by focusing on the repetitions we are able to use them as a mirror to observe our thoughts, emotions, and actions. When we think in terms of repetitive patterns and loops, we can experiment with new ideas and learn by trial and error. We can then use the repetitions to build positive loops and habits.

At a higher level, organizations are caught in their own repetitive loops. Like us, they get stuck too. They have their own realities, which govern the way management and staff interpret the world. In Gareth Morgan's brilliant book, *Images of Organization*,[2] he illustrates how managers use metaphors to make sense of their organizations. These metaphors are organizational versions of "personal realities." One common example is the "machine metaphor," which interprets the organization as a machine where top-down decisions are made and implemented, and everyone follows orders to the letter. Think of a fast-food franchise.

Every organization has its own metaphor or collective reality. The problem is that these realities are often limited and dysfunctional. Reinforced by conformity and "groupthink," these realities can lead to inertia and stagnation.

Just look at the auto industry where General Motors is still churning out gas-guzzling SUVs, while Toyota has overtaken them in worldwide sales with newer, more fuel-efficient cars. When are the big U.S. auto makers going to discard the old paradigm of doing business and embrace hybrid, electric, and hydrogen cars? When are the energy giants going to turn away from oil, gas, and coal and fully commit to renewable energy?

So many large corporations are trapped in their own Groundhog Days, unwilling or unable to break out of the cycle of overconsumption of precious resources, waste, and short-term thinking. Future historians will write with dismay at their failure to act sooner.

Acceptance

The next step is to finally accept that our outdated work habits are no longer working for us. Acceptance is magical because we let go of the enormous tension of trying to be someone we are not. I have a friend, Dave, who was a manager for an investment bank. He became a manager because that was what his peers did, and because he would earn more money.

The problem was that Dave hated being a manager. He wanted to be out winning new business and looking after his clients. He hated being stuck in an office, dealing with a lot of detail and paperwork. He felt trapped for years.

It was only when he divorced that he took time to evaluate what he wanted from his career. He confronted the truth, and accepted that he did not want to be a manager. He went back to sales and rediscovered the magic of doing a job he loved.

Dave suffered some denial, sadness, and even anger. Yet he remained resilient and bounced back from adversity. He allowed his old reality to collapse so a new, healthier one could emerge. Perhaps the hardest step at work is to accept that what we are doing is no longer satisfying; to accept that we are in the wrong business, job, or even career. We hate to admit we are wrong, and that we have wasted time. The commercial world does not seem to suffer admissions of failure very well. In order to save face, we struggle on with the forlorn hope that we can make it better.

Sometimes it is just time to give up. The same is true for organizations themselves. Often the board will just have to face up to the fact that the new product or the new division is not working out. I have had to close businesses that were unsuccessful, and I have had to accept that my strategy and planning were flawed. Over time, this helped me focus on what I was best at, then I could build my business activity around my strengths.

Creativity

As our old reality fades away we are able to create a new one. Our extraordinary capacity for change reveals just how magically creative we can be. When we let go of the past, and escape from our old limiting patterns, we broaden our vision and increase our choices. As we transcend our older, narrow reality we become more open, resourceful, and flexible.

In the constantly changing world of business, this creativity is vital. We no longer have the luxury of one career, and have to continually reinvent ourselves. We must adapt in order to take advantage of the turbulent technological, economic, and organizational currents that move us in many new directions.

None of us can predict the future, and most planning is of little value. Our only power resides in our flexibility. Phil triumphs through his infinite capacity to experiment, monitor, and evaluate the results. He is learns how to live by being creative in his thoughts and behaviors.

I am sure that this experimentation and capacity for learning is the most important skill in the modern workplace. We cannot control the profound changes occurring around us, but we can control our creative responses to these changes. Every day, like Phil, we can choose our strategy. We can choose how to react to our aggressive boss. We can choose how to engage with our most difficult clients. We can experiment with new ways of seeing our jobs, our products and services, our organizations, our customers, and our markets.

Every organization is looking for creative people. Nearly twenty years ago, Peter Senge wrote a seminal book about learning organizations, in which he stressed the need for management to create an environment where everyone is challenging their assumptions, questioning their strategies, and refining their activities.[3]

This is where the magic of Groundhog Day comes into play. It provides the chance to change and experiment with no risk. Phil gets chance after chance to test the impact of his actions. At the end of the day, he goes back to the beginning and tries again. That is a gift a manager can give to his people in order to allow them to develop, and to allow the organization to change in small increments. A good manager will coach her team to learn by doing, to closely observe their thinking and behavior, and to take risks without drastic personal consequences.

When you attain a perpetual state of learning and creative experimentation, you will improve your performance, increase your value, and build a superb career.

Love

Our final stage in shifting to a new personal reality at work is through discovering the magic of love. Now, you might have been with me up to this point, but as soon as the word "love" is applied to work you might raise your eyebrows. What on earth has love got to do with the cut-throat business world?

How do you love your CFO who blocks every new idea you have? How do you love your competitor who badmouths you every chance he gets? It's not easy, but when you don't act with love at work you can be sucked into a vortex of bitterness, fear, and anger.

For many years I knew a business development manager at a telecom business who was eaten up by these negative emotions. She was out to prove that her industry, like nature, was "red in tooth and claw." She seemed caught in a Darwinian struggle for survival, using words like "wounding" and "killing" to describe what she would do to her competition.

This attitude worked fine in the 1980s, and to some extent in the 1990s. Then it began to deliver diminishing returns. She went on courses about serving the customer, interpersonal skills, and emotional intelligence. She sometimes spoke the right words, but her actions always betrayed her aggression. Not only did she alienate her colleagues and her clients, she damaged her health and well-being through constant stress and toxic energy.

All her life she had used negative motivation to drive her forward, whether it was to show her parents that she was better than they gave her credit for, or to let her friends know that she was tougher and more successful than they were. She finally exhausted herself and ran out of steam.

Last summer it all came to a head and she was fired from her job. Forced to confront her career and her life, she went through the same stages as Phil: denial, anger, and finally acceptance. She attended a Buddhist course and discovered a whole new way of thinking about herself. She has gone to work for an NGO, and is focusing her efforts on helping others rather than fighting the competition. She has begun to discover the magic of love, and she is a far happier and healthier person for it.

Indeed, when we add love to the other four types of magic we complete our journey. Love is the missing ingredient that raises us out of our own reality and connects us to the reality of other people and the world at large. As we feel love, we connect to others and find purpose and meaning in our lives.

Imagine doing a job that you love and look forward to every day. Imagine a vocation that embodies your values and allows you to be your authentic self. Imagine if you treated every interaction in the office as an opportunity to practice compassion and help the others feel better about themselves. How would you feel about your career then?

Over the course of our work life we will reap tremendous, life-changing benefits from the moment-to-moment decisions to practice the magic of Groundhog Day. These small decisions mount up to represent the difference between success and failure, between a satisfying and unsatisfying career. As we build a healthy personal reality, we also deal better with workplace stress. A healthy reality improves our physical health too. Research shows that people who are more relaxed, more sociable, and have a clear purpose are happier, healthier, and live longer.[4]

Deciding to Change

Unlike Phil, you do not need thousands of identical days in order to change. It does not matter where you are or who you are with;. Every day is the same blank canvas available to you and on which you can compose a mundane day or a magical day. Our unique human potential lies in our capacity to be aware of each moment and spontaneously choose how to interpret and live it. This is the secret of breaking free of the Groundhog Day Effect. Pay more attention to how you create your day than to the particular occurrences that take place in it. See each day as a new opportunity to create magic.

You can have as much fun as you want with this experiment. You can fill your day with activities that move you toward your goals, or with activities that keep you in your comfort zone. You can fill your day by fixating on what is wrong with your job or by looking for new ideas to make the best of it. If you cannot come up with a way forward, then find a new job. Just do not stay in a rut.

You can fill your day with resenting your work colleagues or connecting with them. You can create your worst day or your best day. This is your authentic magic. There are no tricks or illusions here—and the magic lasts.

It lasts because of the work and practice you invest in it. Phil changes over a long period of repeating time. He is forced to change. Similarly, at work we tend to change in response to a crisis, such as a massive financial loss or a hostile takeover.

Phil learns how to control the way he responds to what is happening, and chooses to engage in voluntary change. So what is *your* trigger for change? You might not be trapped in a time loop, but there might be powerful factors driving you. Maybe you have lost your job or are facing bankruptcy. These are life-changing events that create an urgency to change. Yet as we saw in the chapter on the Groundhog Day Effect, most of us are so habituated to our everyday routine that we cannot even conceive of an alternative, or we deny that one is possible.

The most successful executives and employees do not passively wait for change to happen to them. They are active in the change process, letting uncertainty and complexity work for them rather than paralyze them. They break free of their own Groundhog Day Effect and find their *reason* for changing. They know what is going to motivate them to make the effort and put in the hard work needed. Transformative, sustainable change is very difficult; most people give up along the way.

I have always found that the most successful change programs actively engage the participants. A former client of mine in the UK was a large financial institution where all the managers were being trained in sales. A former initiative had failed because it was neither voluntary nor planned effectively, and the managers felt alienated, with no sense of ownership.

So I spent several weeks meeting with the participants individually and listening to their thoughts about what was happening. Once I understood their hopes and concerns, I was able to build their training around a personalized coaching system rather than generalized lectures. In this way, the managers felt more control and ownership of the change process, and that it was being done "with" them rather than "to" them. They moved from unwilling, reactive subjects of a top-down process to willing, proactive agents of change. Enforced change seldom works or lasts; voluntary change does.

The Principles of Change

There is no right way to change, no simple prescriptive model that has all the answers. What worked for Phil might not work exactly for you, yet there are a number of insights and principles worth applying. These are based on *Groundhog Day* and supported by my own experience, from over twenty-five years of working with change at the individual, group, and organizational level. If you want to finish the journey from a bad day to magical day, you will face many challenges. The following principles will help.

Change Takes a Long Time

Change places demands on us, and most people do not voluntarily change their personal reality. A struggle ensues, so that we rarely enjoy a seamless transition. Repetition and practice are critical. Creating a healthier reality means

forming new habits, which takes a long time. We cannot
find shortcuts here. It takes Phil many years to change and
it might take you the same.

One way of dealing with long time spans is to break
down your journey into months, weeks, and days. Keep a
journal that records your progress. Psychologists studying
happiness ask research participants to keep a "daily recon-
struction journal" in which they record their moods and
psychological states in detail throughout the day.[5]

The magic of Groundhog Day works when you pay
attention and let the repetition work for you. Think of each
day as a separate unit of time. You can transform your performance and career day by day. Each day, focus on a single behavioral goal. On Monday you could focus on not
judging your colleagues. Intensely focus on the present
moment and notice when a judgmental thought arises and
the feelings that go with it. Then stop the thought and
replace it with a more positive one.

You will see the changes as they happen, but don't
expect results straight away. Phil only has a day to see the
results of his behavior, because the next day he will wake
up and nobody else will remember what he did. We have
more time and can see the results accumulate. The key is to
measure the change and record the day-to-day improvements.

Practice will make perfect. The more you catch and
stop yourself in conditioned responses, the more you will
change your behaviors. It is hard work because all the time

the gravity of your personal reality will be pulling you back down to your familiar reactions and thinking patterns. Over time, however, you will create new, more positive habits. These habits will form the backbone of the new, transformed you.

Be Resilient

The journey is rarely direct or simple. There are lots of detours and wrong turns along the way. Often you think you have changed when, in fact, you have not. Phil has to go through many wrong turns before he finally escapes, and so will you. He reverts to type, to his default personal reality. Are you the same? Do you change for a while, then revert to default mode?

At the outset of organizational change programs there is often rapid progress. Participants enjoy some early successes, but then get bogged down by difficult challenges. Most managers I have known are mercurial. They are dynamic in the good times, but gravity brings them back to their old, comfortable personal reality during the hard times. They continue to go round in the same old circles, and stay stuck for a long time while deluding themselves that they have moved on.

Resilient people are very successful. The best manager I ever worked with always took on the tough issues. She always acknowledged and faced her fears head-on, never avoiding hardships that most of us would shirk from. For example, she had a lifelong dread of public speaking, so whenever she had to give a group presentation she would practice and rehearse for countless hours. Never would she back out, because she knew that her power came from constantly taking on what she most feared.

While her colleagues spent hours every day avoiding tough tasks, engaged in endless meetings and planning exercises, she always did what needed to be done. With tremendous self-discipline and courage she outpaced them all, and became the first female executive of her corporation.

Be Wary of "Definitive" Maps

One of the advantages of *Groundhog Day* is that it shows where different directions lead. We can see what happens when Phil tries different paths — first a hedonistic lifestyle, then a life based on serving others.

Whereas Phil's experiences offer a basic map to guide you, it is not a definitive map. I doubt whether such a map exists, despite the claims of many business gurus and organizations to possess one. There are many ways to progress on your journey.

Phil does not have a guide, a book, or a doctrine to lead him. He has to navigate his own way and travel by trial and error. I believe that such an experiential approach is best. Do not trust someone else's word; try it out for yourself. If you like some of the ideas in this book, test them to make sure they are right for you. Make your own choices and develop your own path.

At work, this means taking charge of our careers and

adhering to our own values and beliefs. Naturally, we need to fit into the organizational culture and conform to corporate practices. The problem emerges when we stop thinking for ourselves, and create our own loops of slavishly following what is politically correct. Leaders are autonomous, free thinking, and self-determined.

Be Prepared

Phil has every day to do nothing but focus on making the journey, and you will need to find time to do the same. If you are going to genuinely change, get moving and do it. Make the commitment and do the work. Even if you feel tired or downhearted, make the effort to effect small changes and build some momentum.

Perhaps the most important preparation of all is to ensure that you are in the right state of mind. You might not know the exact route, and you will make mistakes along the way. You cannot control everything, but you can control your state of mind. The more you remain calm, monitor your thoughts, and pay attention to what is going on around you, the easier the journey will be.[6]

You Can Start the Journey Whenever and Wherever You Want

At first, Phil is in denial about his situation. It is only when he acknowledges what is happening to him that he starts trying to change. So if you believe you are stuck, get going now. Do not wait until everything is ready, since it never will be. Every day is a learning experience, a chance to try new thoughts and new behaviors. This is a journey that you can start whenever you want and wherever you are.

Do Not Announce to the World, "I have changed!"
Phil does not go around at the end telling Rita and everyone else that he has changed. He lets his actions speak for themselves. If you advertise your "transformation," you are setting yourself up for a fall. All your colleagues at the office will be looking for a chance to bring you down to earth.

If you promise a great deal and then fail to deliver, you are worse off than before. Do not expect everyone else to believe you have changed, or even to believe that what you are doing is important. Some people might even be unhappy that you are changing, because it puts them on the spot. Just focus on living each moment as you want to and let others see and say what they want to.

You Have to Keep Working at It
Never rest on your laurels. If you want the magical day to turn into a magical life, the work will never be complete. The journey is the point, not the destination. We don't know what the future holds for Phil on February 4, 5, 6, and

beyond. Maybe he has reached a state of permanent enlightenment. I do not know, but I suspect that without careful vigilance he may slip back into some of his old ways.

If we were able to see into Phil's future, quite possibly we would observe him drifting in and out of the Groundhog Day Effect. Perhaps there is a natural cycle at work? Or perhaps Phil has to go through every possible choice, every experience, to get to where he is on the last day in the time loop. Perhaps there is a time for everything and the time for Phil to be transformed or "self-actualized" is on that final day.

Do Not Become Obsessed with Change

Phil changes naturally; he never tries to force changes on himself. By the end of the movie he has a relaxed, playful attitude, entirely authentic to his personality. He is not trying to project an image. He is just doing and being what comes naturally.

So be careful about setting specific outcomes or being too tough on yourself. You could even end up creating a personal reality that is dependent on constant change and improvement. You may know people who are addicted to self-help books. I do, and these folks bounce around from one uncompleted program to another. Nothing alters as they stay trapped in their new loop.

Simply enjoy the moment as Phil does. Accept that there are probably many things you will not be able to change.

Dance with life; don't fight it. Enjoy each day for its own value rather than as a building block toward your goals.

Time is our greatest gift and our greatest teacher. Phil is forced to consider the meaning and value of time during his stay in Punxsutawney. When you do the same, you raise the hope and the possibility that you can turn today and tomorrow into magical days. This is the magic of *Groundhog Day.*

Conclusion

Spreading the Magic

In this final chapter, I want to tie all the themes of this book together and describe the big picture. So far, I have written about our individual patterns of repetitive thoughts and behaviors and offered some ideas for breaking free of them, at home and work. Now I want to raise the stakes and offer you a far more important and urgent reason for making changes in your life.

I believe that the magic of Groundhog Day is a philosophy that can guide us in every area of our lives. It integrates every dimension of the human experience, because everything that Phil Connors experiences is relevant to us as individuals, families, organizations, and societies. Furthermore, we cannot confine ourselves to a town like Punxsutawney, frozen in time and place. Our world is open, complex, and dependent on many connections that shape everything we do. When we see and understand these connections, we have to adopt a much broader perspective.

Groundhog Day on Planet Earth

You and I are part of a civilization that is caught in its own Groundhog Day, stuck in repetitive patterns of collective thinking and behavior that threaten the future survival of the human race.

Our institutions are suffering from the Groundhog Day Effect. Businesses are trapped by the need to avoid risk and achieve short-term profits. Governments are trapped by the demands of spin, lobbyists, and electoral pressures, unable to solve fundamental long-term problems like health care and education. Society is trapped by the conventional wisdom that individual prosperity and economic growth are the answers to everything.

Hundreds of millions of people are trapped by poverty, by conflict, by a lack of basic human rights, and by oppressive regimes.[1] They are prisoners of their circumstances, yet the "magic" they yearn for is very simple. It is satisfying basic needs like finding work, supporting their families, and enjoying peace, democracy, justice, health, and education.

Millions of people in the developed countries are ensnared in the Groundhog Day Effect. In the United States, most people are commuting and working longer hours to pay for more things that are making them less happy. They are spending less time with their kids, while building up huge debts for these same kids to be educated to live the same way!

Most serious of all, every one of us is marooned on a planet that is heading toward environmental catastrophe. Our civilization is unsustainable. We are going round faster and faster in circles while approaching the edge of a cliff. If we do not halt global warming very soon, we risk making our planet uninhabitable.

You might be thinking, "What on earth has all this got to do with a Hollywood comedy released in the 1990s?" The simple answer is that our civilization is stuck in its own Groundhog Day, and it is taking us on a one-way trip to disaster.

I want to devote this concluding chapter to exploring how we can change and, in particular, tackle our massive environmental problems. I want to focus on environmental problems because they present the greatest challenge facing humanity. We have to find answers—and soon—as the scale and severity of our predicament is overwhelming. Our challenges include species extinction, deforestation, sea pollution, desertification, topsoil reduction, and freshwater depletion. The potential consequences of our current direction are alarming, and include ecological collapse, major conflict, famine, drought, and economic depression.

The Global Groundhog Day Effect

We are repeating destructive patterns of unbridled growth based on fossil fuels, and we are suffering from the delusional idea that economic growth and rising consumption are the answers to everything. Entranced in a collective Groundhog Day Effect, we are all living on automatic pilot as we drift toward ecological oblivion.

The majority of people are focused on their personal and family interests without realizing that their well-being ultimately depends on the well-being of our ecosystems. We might be aware of the problem, yet we feel stuck and powerless to do anything about it. We blame business and governments, while these institutions say there are not enough votes or profits to do anything significant about the problem.

As with our individual patterns of behavior, the cause of our problem lies with our personal reality or, rather, the aggregation of millions of individual realities that make up our "collective reality" or worldview. Our realities are largely concerned with our individual needs, and our worldviews reflect this. We are repeating the same patterns at a group, organizational, national, and global level.

A Dangerous Collective Reality

We might differ in race, nationality, religion, and culture. We might differ in personality, education, and upbringing. Yet most of us share certain assumptions about the world that form our collective reality and, though largely unconscious, influence and shape individual lifestyles, corporate activities, and government policy.

These assumptions include the view that we humans are separate from nature. We behave as though we are the only significant species on this planet. The rest of nature is simply there to be exploited for our needs. Another assumption is that our primary goal in life is to consume more. We measure our success by how many possessions we have and by their value. Similarly, we assume that we are only responsible for ourselves and our families, and are too busy to think of the bigger global issues. Mired in this narrow worldview, we are disconnected from each other and from nature.

Consequently, we make decisions based on economic considerations while ignoring the environmental costs. Our worldview thrives on self-interest and, in the developed countries, on rampant consumerism reinforced by big business, the markets, and the media. Motivated by self-absorption, greed, competition, and status, we are destroying our planet, and we are no happier for it.

We have let the corporations substitute their own *artificial* needs for our *authentic* needs. According to Chilean economist Max-Neef, we are entranced by "pseudo-satisfiers."[2] These are possessions or achievements that satisfy us temporarily, giving us feelings of power or status, but that do not address our authentic needs for love and meaning.

Modern consumer lifestyles are designed around these pseudo-satisfiers. Luxury goods are a classical example.

When you go to Rodeo Drive in Los Angeles or Bond Street in London you can be intoxicated by the experience. Like a drug, it gives you a temporary high. A beautiful young person beckons you in. Captivated by the stunning displays and the attentive sales assistant, you end up paying $250 for a shirt with a particular label, which you do not need but which gives you a quick euphoric burst of power and status

You are not improving the quality of your life, since you are not satisfying a real need. Earlier, I referred to these authentic needs and the positive psychology literature that has proven money to be *less important* to our level of happiness than friendship, community, or meaningful work. Despite these findings, we as individuals and organizations behave otherwise. Our worldview is a dangerous delusion that is both obscuring and eroding the real magic of our world. As with unhealthy personal realities, we can contrast our current unhealthy worldview with a vision of a healthy worldview.

I believe that the magic of *Groundhog Day* could work at a collective level too. Phil changes when he discovers the magic in his life. We are more likely to change when we discover the magic in our lives and in our world.

Paying Attention to the Earth

We have the knowledge and the technology needed to make progress. There are significant new initiatives to design businesses, housing, and transportation in harmony with nature. A good example is the city of Portland, Oregon, regularly voted the greenest city in the United States. According to my friends who live there, Portland is a wonderful community because it integrates the needs of its citizens with the needs of the environment. It has great public transportation, cycling and walking paths; it has excellent water; and it has cut back greenhouse gas emissions. The citizens of Portland commute less, save on energy costs, and are healthier.

The city still has a long way to go to be a blueprint for sustainability. Yet it offers a vision of how we can live more healthy and fulfilling lives while consuming less resources and reducing our ecological footprint.[3] At a time when we continually hear what is wrong with the environment, Portland offers hope for the future and leads the way in showing how change is possible.[4]

These ideas will only take root when more of us pay attention to the ecosystems that give us life. Then we can fully appreciate the magic of our world, and build magical towns and cities. Phil has to leave his world in order to appreciate it. He has to make a fundamental change to his reality in order to rediscover the magic of life. Imagine if you were to do the same.

Imagine that instead of being caught in a time loop for thousands of days, you are lost in space for the same time. Stuck in your spacecraft, every day feels the same. You have seen nothing but lifeless planets and asteroids for what seems like an eternity. Then you wake up one morning and glimpse Earth for the first time since you left. As you come closer, you feel overwhelmed by its beauty. You are in awe at the colors, the different landscapes, the clouds, the light, and the oceans.

You remember Yuri Gagarin's words after his first spaceflight in 1961: "When I orbited the Earth in a spaceship, I saw for the first time how beautiful our planet is. Mankind, let us preserve and increase this beauty, and not destroy it!"[5] As you come back into the atmosphere you move past rainforests, mountains, and wilderness. You are tearful with relief and joy at the magic around you—the majestic peaks, lakes, and flowing rivers.

Then you land and are taken to a city. You see the ugly buildings with unhappy people rushing around in circles. You see roads choked with cars. You see factories and power plants scarring the landscape. You contemplate the contrast between the magnificence of Earth from space, and humanity's indifference to it. You are disturbed by all the resources consumed by this city, by the buried toxic waste, by all the pollution and carbon emissions being poured into the atmosphere. Then you ask yourself, "How could we have done this to our unique, wonderful planet?"

This might be science fiction, but it illustrates an important point. If you were to be transported away from your familiar routine and banished from Earth for many years, you would never take our planet for granted again. You would pay attention to what we are doing to our world and feel guilty, shocked, and distressed.

Hypnotized by our repetitive, unsustainable lifestyle, we fail to see the big picture. We do not appreciate the beauty or the fragility of our planet, and fail to see the consequences of our toxic lifestyle. We deceive ourselves with the dangerous rationalization "out of sight, out of mind." When we drive and fly, we do not see the pollution and carbon emissions. When we use cleaning products in our homes, we do not see the release of harmful chemicals. When we eat meat, we do not see the death of the cow or the ecological cost of getting the meal to our table.

Nature's Repetitions

Western lifestyles conceal the magic of our existence by separating us from nature. We miss the repetitions, or rhythms, of nature such as the changing seasons. We have built a civilization that exploits nature and ignores its deeper patterns. We are living on automatic pilot, locked in to an unsustainable lifestyle. We rely on oil, gas, and coal to heat our homes and provide electricity. We rely on gas for our automobiles and aviation fuel for jet travel. We rely on huge amounts of energy to obtain our food and all the other products we consume without a second thought.

Fortunately, we do have alternatives. We can largely depend on local food and live in tune with the natural cycles of the seasons. In my local community, we buy all our fruit and vegetables from an organic farm only three miles from our home. This helps the environment by eliminating the transportation of food from around the world, provides work for the community, and improves our health because the food is organic.

The Slow Food Movement embodies these principles. Set up in Italy in 1989, it consists of people and organizations around the globe dedicated to conserving local food traditions and slowing down the pace of life. Their philosophy is that "Slow Food is good, clean and fair food. We believe that the food we eat should taste good; that it should be produced in a clean way that does not harm the environment, animal welfare or our health."[6]

Slow Food has now given birth to the Slow Cities or "Cittaslow" movement. Slow cities offer us the possibility of breaking free from patterns of locked-in behavior. They promote the integration of public transport, green buildings, locally produced organic food, and active community participation. According to their UK website, "The aim of a Cittaslow is to encourage people to live and enjoy life at a human pace, and to provide an infrastructure that helps people savor and enjoy life and what it has to offer."[7]

Accepting the Necessity for Change

I believe strongly that the mission of Slow Food and Slow Cities is to help us accept what we have lost, and also what is most important for the happiness and health of our families. In *Groundhog Day,* Phil gains a new perspective when he moves from the big city to the small town; from the high-pressure career to a slower pace; from complexity to simplicity. He discovers that the best things in life are free, finding meaning and fulfillment in authentic relationships and being part of a community.

For many people, the film arouses a nostalgic longing for a lost world: a world where people are genuine, caring, and happy, a world that works at a slower pace and where the important qualities are truly valued, a world that is friendly and safe. More and more people are seeking this lost world though lifestyle choices such as downshifting and voluntary simplicity.[8]

One of the happiest people I know downshifted five years ago. My friend was a highflyer in Wall Street, earning a seven-figure salary and living in a chic apartment in an upscale neighborhood of Manhattan. He and his wife drove luxury cars, had a second home in Vermont, and took expensive vacations in the Caribbean.

On the surface, everything was perfect. They were living the American dream. Beneath the surface, though, my friend was deeply unhappy. He spent his days with people he despised and doing work he hated. One weekend he confided his unhappiness to his wife, who had reached the same conclusion herself. Within a week, he resigned from his job and they put their apartment up for sale.

They moved to their two-bedroom home in rural Vermont. He took up writing, while she started to play the piano and paint. He will never be the next Ernest Hemingway, nor she the next Georgia O'Keefe. It doesn't matter. They accepted what really mattered in their lives, and took up activities they loved for their own sake. They decided that time was their greatest asset, and they wanted to invest their time in meaningful and enjoyable activities, not in maintaining their expensive Manhattan lifestyle.

They cut their spending by 70 percent, and dramatically improved their physical and psychological health. They became active in their community, made friends who did not care where they lived or what they owned, and their relationship together was as fresh and exciting as before they married. They felt free for the first time in their lives. They could no longer accept the noise, rush, and overstimulation of Manhattan and wondered why they had not made the break ten years earlier.

In many ways, they were following a long tradition. For thousands of years, religious leaders have been advocating a simple life dedicated to family, friends, community, and nature. They did not seek a simpler lifestyle because it was good for the environment or because it was trendy. No, they sought simplicity because it improved the quality of their lives immeasurably.

Even if we do not dramatically change our lives, we all need to accept that we need to change. In developed countries, we find it difficult to accept the truth for many reasons. Some people do not know the facts; many more know them but choose to ignore them because they do not seem relevant to their everyday lives. We frequently deny the seriousness of the danger involved, or we project all the blame onto government or big business. We talk about the environment in abstract, detached terms and rarely engage emotionally with the issues, which is why we often fail to take action.

It is hard to accept the truth. When I first learned the facts about the current state of our planet, I became over-whelmed with anxiety. My initial reaction was to give up and "head for the hills." Many people who become aware of our predicament feel the same. The scale and complexity of the crisis are beyond anything we have faced before. Denial or resignation is an understandable response.

Once we accept that nature is suffering and humans are suffering, we can accept responsibility for this suffering, and be better prepared to meet the challenge. Once we accept this, we can choose to live more sustainably and better protect our very own life-support systems. More-over, Slow Food, Slow Cities, and Voluntary Simplicity provide us with the tools and techniques to live more sus-tainably, healthily, and joyfully. Maybe there is a way for-ward?

Creating a Sustainable Future

Once we accept responsibility, the next step is to develop creative solutions to our problems. This means limiting or stopping the invention of unsustainable products and the exploration for new oilfields — and redirecting our creativity, effort, and resources into sustainable technologies and renewable energies.

Creativity means making the connections between sustainability and our everyday needs and concerns. As an individual, you can make connections between protecting the environment and every aspect of your lifestyle. When you walk instead of drive, you use less gas, save money, and improve your fitness. When you buy ecological products for your home, you protect your family from harmful toxins. When you work on a local conservation program, you protect your local ecosystem and gain all the proven benefits of community building, volunteering, and friendship.

Organizations can make connections between reducing energy and waste and increasing profitability, and between sustainable products and exciting business opportunities. It is possible that the demand for renewable energy and green products and services could create the biggest market in history.

In their recent book *The Clean Tech Revolution*,[9] authors Ron Pernick and Clint Wilder give us the facts and the predictions about this massive opportunity. They highlight research that shows that the global biofuels market will increase from $20.5 billion in 2006 to $80.9 billion by 2016; the wind power market from $17.9 billion in 2006 to $60.8 billion in 2016; and solar power from $15.6 billion in 2006 to $69.3 billion in 2016.[10] General Electric alone through its ecomagination initiative, launched in 2005, achieved sales of "green" products, including wind power and clean coal, of $12 billion in 2006. CEO Jeff Immelt was quoted as saying, "Ecomagination is growing beyond our expectations, evolving into a sales initiative unlike any other I've seen in 25 years at GE."11

On a smaller scale, we find the example of the New Belgium Brewery in Fort Collins, Colorado12. The founders, husband-and-wife team Jeff Lebesch and Kim Jordan, have applied rigorous sustainable practices to dramatically reduce waste, conserve energy, and save water. They power their plant with a combination of wind power and methane, and also adhere to strict green building standards. A third of their workforce typically cycle to work, and they have a strong employee ownership program. In many ways, this is a "magical business" where employees can integrate their livelihoods with finding meaning, connection, and environmental stewardship.

Businesses can spread magic just like individuals. This would happen a lot more frequently if they enjoyed government support through new policies, laws, and tax breaks. Governments can promote the relationship between the welfare of their citizens and the welfare of their ecosystems. For example, when governments pass laws to protect the environment and clean up the air and water, they improve public health and reduce health-care costs.

When governments provide incentives for environmental entrepreneurs, they promote jobs and growth. And when governments support renewable energy with tax cuts and legislation, they become less dependent on oil from dangerous regions and promote national security.

Environmental Leadership

There has been a massive increase in media coverage and awareness of climate change over the last few years. What we now need is leadership that will turn our awareness and anxiety into the will to take action, and then follow through with long-term solutions. At every level, from communities and businesses to national governments and the United Nations, we need creative leaders more that at any time in our history.

Indeed, I have decided to focus my efforts on identifying and supporting environmental leaders. I decided that I needed to do more than teach and write. I needed to take action, and that meant using my entrepreneurial experience and skills to be an environmental leader myself. So earlier this year, I set up a new business in London called Bright Green Talent www.brightgreentalent.com with a young entrepreneur I met at Oxford, Tom Savage. Tom was voted the UK's young social entrepreneur of the year in 2007, and is an environmental leader himself.

We have both decided that the best use of our time, energies, and skills is to recruit current and future environmental leaders for our clients on both sides of the Atlantic.

We work with corporations, start-ups, NGOs, and government agencies with a strong commitment to the environment and corporate social responsibility. We have also set up an office in California, and we are encouraging the brightest and best of our respective generations to dedicate their careers to promoting sustainability.

In many ways, we have created Bright Green as the embodiment of the *Groundhog Day* principles. We want to build a "magical organization" full of people who are looking for meaning and purpose in their work. And we want to help organizations to improve society and our planet.

We believe that people want more than just a paycheck from their work. And we believe that, to achieve their full potential, employees need a cause that is greater than their own self-interest. Even if you do not directly work in this sector, the point is that wherever you work or live, you can make a difference. Even if you do not save a falling boy, you can still save a tree. There are a thousand creative ways to save energy and avoid waste. Simply visit this book's website to learn how.13

Loving Our Earth

Environmental leaders are motivated by feelings of connection and love for the earth. Phil changes when he discovers the magic of love, and so can we. One of the great challenges facing the environmental movement has been to engage the public emotionally. We care for what and who we love, particularly our partners and family. When we love the earth in the same way, we will care for it too.

Without love, the environment remains an abstract concept. If you live in the middle of Manhattan, and your life revolves around Wall Street and Fifth Avenue, you are detached from the natural world. It is hard to experience a loving bond to nature.

When we care for the environment, we also care for our fellow human beings. We are all bound together in a complex system, and we are all responsible for each other and the other species with which we share the planet.

> Everyone shares responsibility for the present and future well-being of the human family and the larger living world. The spirit of human solidarity and kinship with all life is strengthened when we live with reverence for the mystery of being, gratitude for the gift of life, and humility regarding the human place in nature.
>
> — Earth Charter[14]

We are part of nature. Our well-being ultimately depends on the well-being of our ecosystems, which support life itself. When we love our planet, we take responsibility and are accountable for our actions. Living sustainably means being compassionate to all species, and this includes humans. When we live sustainably, we are looking after current and future generations. We are acting as stewards, accountable to our children and grandchildren.

Phil only discovers joy and meaning through loving other people and life itself. Phil helps himself by helping others. Furthermore, we can add a third dimension to this. With a little imagination we can satisfy our personal needs, the needs of others, and also our ecological needs

We can change from being selfish consumers, acting out of misguided self-interest, and become concerned citizens, working for the good of others and the planet. There are simple, elegant strategies available to us now. We can develop a sustainable worldview and lifestyle built on the following proven principles of individual happiness:

- Optimism that we can find solutions to the environmental crisis
- Meaning and purpose from working as stewards of the earth
- Reducing stress through downshifting and voluntary simplicity
- Improved health and fitness from organic food, more walking and cycling
- Sense of belonging to a community by working near home, buying from farmers' markets, and encouraging local businesses and agriculture
- Volunteering for environmental NGOs and joining local conservation programs

These are achievable changes that will reconnect us with the magic of our world. When we reconnect like this, we ensure that we improve our well-being as well as the well-being of other people, other species, and our ecosystems.[15]

Every decision we make has an enormous effect on the world. The daily decisions of 6.5 billion people determine the future of the human race. If we go back to the idea of Old and New Phil, we can compare what a world populated by each one would be like. This is not to say that New Phil would be an environmentalist, though he is more likely to be than the old one. New Phil genuinely cares for humanity, and the welfare of humanity is synonymous with the welfare of the environment.

In many ways, Old Phil was an adolescent. He was self-absorbed and thought little about the consequences of his actions. Teenagers crave instant gratification and are fiercely independent. New Phil, by contrast, is a mature, self-actualized adult. He thinks carefully about his actions, behaves responsibly. and serves others.

The dominant worldview of our civilization closely resembles adolescence.[16] Our culture is built on individualism, competition, instant gratification. and disregard for the consequences of our lifestyle. We crave pleasure and assert our individual rights above collective responsibility.

So what would happen if we all went through a similar process to Phil? How would the world be different? If we follow through the implications of Phil's transformation, we can see that he provides important insights about how we should live. The self-actualized Phil is more connected to the world, more loving, and more responsible. It seems a logical next step for him to care about the world beyond Punxsutawney.

Indeed, the most important lesson for the environmental movement is that Phil changes his behavior naturally as a result of profound emotional, even spiritual change. He is not loving because he has learned the facts about the psychological benefits of love, and he is not helping people because someone has told him to or passed a law. No, he has changed because he wants to. It is entirely authentic.

This is also the key to environmental change. Sustainable behaviors need to be meaningful and authentic. Then we can have it all. As we have seen in this chapter, we can earn our living engaged in meaningful work in environmentally and socially responsible corporations. We can enjoy the health benefits of local food and greener communities. And we can reduce stress and find joy by living more simply.

The Magic of Groundhog Day shows how we can break free of our unhealthy patterns and change to new healthy patterns. If we were to change like Phil, we would be more content. And if we were to collectively change, we could build a better society. We would be happier, we would help other people to be happier, and we would care for our planet. This is the greatest magic of all, and one that takes us on an exciting new journey from a magical life to a magical world.

Notes

⁓

Chapter 1: The Groundhog Day Effect

1. For a good overview of this dysfunctional pattern of consumption, see Gregg Easterbrook, *The Progress Paradox: How Life Gets Better While People Feel Worse* New York: Random House, 2003, Robert H. Frank, *Luxury Fever: Why Money Fails to Satisfy in an Era of Excess* Princeton: Princeton University Press, 2000, and P. C Whybrow, *American Mania: When More Is Not Enough* New York: W. W. Norton, 2005.

2. See P. D. Ouspensky, *The Psychology of Man's Possible Evolution* New York: Hedgehog Press, 1950.

Chapter 3: The Magic of Paying Attention

1. C. G. Jung, *Memories, Dreams, Reflections*. New York: Pantheon 1961.

2. Fred B. Bryant and Joseph Veroff, *Savoring: A New Model of*

Positive Experience Mahwah, NJ: Lawrence Erlbaum Associates, 2006.

3. Martin Seligman, *Authentic Happiness* New York: Free Press, 2002.

4. J. Kabat-Zinn, Wherever You Go, There You Are: Mindfulness Meditation in Everyday Life Hyperion, New York 1994.

Chapter 4: The Magic of Repetition

1. W.R. Torbert, *The Power of Balance: Transforming Self, Society, and Scientific Inquiry* Newbury Park: Sage, 1991

    C. Argyris and D. Schön, *Theory in Practice: Increasing Professional Effectiveness* San Francisco: Jossey-Bass, 1974[P1]

Chapter 5: The Magic of Acceptance

1. See Elisabeth Kübler-Ross, *On Death and Dying* Macmillan, NY 1969.

2. See S. Lyubomirsky and C. Tkach, "The Consequences of Dysphoric Rumination" in *Rumination: Nature, Theory, and Treatment of Negative Thinking in Depression,* C. Papageorgiou and A. Wells, eds. Chichester, England: John Wiley & Sons, 2003.

3. An introduction to Alcoholics Anonymous is available on their website: http://www.alcoholics-anonymous.org/en_pdfs/p-42_abriefguidetoaa.pdf

4. For information about ACT, see Steven C. Hayes and Spencer Smith, *Get Out of Your Mind and Into Your Life: The New Acceptance and Commitment Therapy* New Harbinger Publications, 2005.

5. See St. John of the Cross, *Dark Night of the Soul,* E. Allison Peers, trans. New York: Image Books, 1959.

6. See S. Nolen-Hoeksema and C. G. Davis, "Positive Responses to Loss: Perceiving Benefits and Growth in *Handbook of Positive Psychology,* C. R. Snyder and S. Lopez, eds. New York: Oxford University Press, 2002.
    See M. M. Tugade and B. L. Fredrickson, "Resilient Individuals Use Positive Emotions to Bounce Back from Negative Emotional Experiences," *Journal of Personality and Social Psychology* 86 2004: 320–333.

7. From "Deceptions" in Philip Larkin, *Collected Poems* London: Faber and Faber, 1998.

8. See Richard Feynman, *QED: The Strange Theory of Light and Matter* Princeton University Press, 1985.

9. For a good overview of how to identify your strengths and build a career on them, see the following book, which is supported by extensive research from the Gallup Organization. Marcus Buckingham and Donald O. Clifton, *Now, Discover Your Strengths* New York: Free Press, 2001.

10. From "The Life with a Hole in It,"Philip Larkin, *Collected Poems* London: Faber and Faber, 1998.

11 There has been a great deal of research into the physical and psychological benefits of forgiveness. A useful summary is found in the following book, written by a former director of the pioneering Stanford Forgiveness Project. Frederic Luskin, *Forgive for Good* San Francisco: Harper, 2001.

12. A fascinating if controversial study into the effects of near-death experiences NDE was published in 2001 by Dutch researchers. Their study suggests that the people who expe-

rienced NDE underwent a transformative spiritual experience: P. van Lommel, R. van Wees, V. Meyers, and I. Elf-
ferich, "Near-Death Experience in Survivors of Cardiac
Arrest: A Prospective Study in the Netherlands," *The Lancet*
358 2001: 9298, 2039–2044.

Chapter 6: The Magic of Creativity

1. See Mihaly Csikszentmihalyi, *Flow: The Psychology of Optimal
   Experience* New York: Harper and Row, 1990.

2. Helen Keller's life provides perhaps the most extraordinary
   example of how you can overcome any limits with the right
   attitude, determination, and work ethic. You can read her
   autobiography, *The Story of My Life*, online at
   http://www.gutenberg.org/etext/2397.

Chapter 7: The Magic of Love

1. A major research program into this area is being under-
   taken at the Institute for Research on Unlimited Love,
   School of Medicine Case Western Reserve University
   http://www.unlimitedloveinstitute.org/welcome/index.html.
   See also H. Fisher, *Why We Love: The Nature and Chemistry of
   Romantic Love* New York: Henry Holt, 2004.

2. See P. A. Thoits and L. N. Hewitt, "Volunteer Work and
   Well-being," *Journal of Health and Social Behavior* 2001:
   42:115–131, S. L. Brown, R. M. Nesse, A. D. Vinokur, and
   D. M. Smith, "Providing Social Support May Be More
   Beneficial Than Receiving It: Results from a Prospective
   Study of Mortality," in *Psychological Science* 14 2001:

320–327, and J. A. Pliavin, "Doing Well by Doing Good: Benefits for the Benefactor in *Flourishing: The Positive Psychology and the Life Well Lived,* Corey Lee M. Keyes and Jon Haidt, eds. Washington, DC:APA, 2003.

3. See Victor Frankl, *Man's Search For Meaning* Boston: Beacon Press, 2006.

4. See Robert D. Putnam, *Bowling Alone: The Collapse and Revival of American Community* New York: Simon & Schuster, 2000.

5. See D. G. Myers, "The Funds, Friends, and Faith of Happy People, *American Psychologist* 55 2000: 56–67 and D. Myers, "Close Relationships and the Quality of Life" in *Well-being: The foundations of Hedonic Psychology,* D. Kahneman, E. Diener, and N. Schwarz , eds. New York: Russell Sage Foundation, 1999

6. See J. McPherson, Lynn Smith-Lovin Miller, and Matthew E. Brashears, "Social Isolation in America: Changes in Core Discussion Networks over Two Decades," *American Sociological Review* 71[3] June 2006: 353–375.

Chapter 8: A Magical Life

1. *Siddhartha* 1922 by Herman Hesse is available online at http://www.gutenberg.org/etext/2500
    The Odyssey by Homer is available online at http://www.gutenberg.org/etext/1727

2. Nietzsche, Frederick: translated by Walter Kaufmann; *Thus Spoke Zarathustra: A Book for All and None*; New York, Modern Library 1995
    In his book *Strange Tale of Ivan Osokin* P.D Ouspensky deals with the idea of eternal recurrence, and suggests that we

can only escape the phenomenon by finding meaning in our lives.

Ouspensky, P.D; *Strange Life of Ivan Osokin* New York and London: Holme, 1947

3.   Marino, Gordon 2004 *Basic Writings of Existentialism* Modern Library Classics

4.   See *Aristotle's Nicomachean Ethics:* Available online at http://etext.library.adelaide.edu.au/a/aristotle/nicomachean/

5.   For an introduction to Solipsism see: Wood, Ledger, "Solipsism", in Runes Ed., *Dictionary of Philosophy:* New Jersey, Littlefield, Adams, and Company 1962.

6.   *Maya* — the illusion that our physical world is the only reality

Nirvana — when the soul is released from the cycle of birth and death to reach a state of great peace and contentment

7.   For a description of the movie series see: http://www.moma.org/exhibitions/film_media/2003/hidden_god.html

8.   Dukkha *The Buddhism concept that our normal state of mind creates suffering*

9.   Satori: The Zen Buddhist term for "awakening" from one's dream.

10. Maslow, A. H. Self-actualizing people: A study of psychological health. In C. E. Moustakas Ed., *The self: Explorations in personal growth*. New York: Harper & Row 1956

11. Jung, C.G. *The Integration of the Personality.*, London: Kegan Paul, Trench, Trubner &Co 1940.

12. Erikson 1997. Phil's development can also be characterized

as a progress in values from "self-enhancement" to "self-transcendence"; from power and achievement to benevolence and "universalism."

Schwartz, S.H. Universals in the content and structure of values: Theoretical advances and empirical tests in 20 countries. *Advances in Experimental Social Psychology*, M. Zanna ed., San Diego: Academic Press 1992.

13. Miller, W. R., & C'de Baca, J. *Quantum change: When epiphanies and sudden insights transform ordinary lives*. New York: Guilford Press 2001.

14. See Daniel Gilbert's essay online at
http://www.edge.org/3rd_culture/gilbert03/gilbert_index.html
For further evidence that money does not buy you happiness see: *Would You Be Happier If You Were Richer? A Focusing Illusion*. D. Kahneman, A. B. Krueger, D. Schkade, N. Schwarz, and A. A. Stone 2006.
Frank, R. H. 2004. "How Not to Buy Happiness." Daedalus 133[2]: 69-79.

15. Gilbert, Daniel "Stumbling on Happiness," Canada, Knopf 2006.

16. See Seligman 2002 and Haidt, J, *The happiness hypothesis: Finding modern truth in ancient wisdom* New York: Basic Books 2006.

17. Ryan, R. M., & Deci, E. L. An overview of self-determination theory. In E. L. Deci & R. M. Ryan Eds., *Handbook of self-determination research* pp. 3-33. Rochester, NY: University of Rochester Press 2002.
Sheldon, K.M., & Elliot A.J. 1999. Goal striving, need-sat-

isfaction, and longitudinal well-being: The Self-Concor-
dance Model. *Journal of Personality and Social Psychology,* 76,
482-497.

18. For a summary of such irrational attitudes see Ellis, Albert
A New Guide to Rational Living. Englewood Cliffs: Prentice
Hall NJ 1975.

Chapter 9 A Magical Career

1. For an overview see my first book which I co-wrote with
John Selby. Hannam P.D, Selby .J: *Take Charge of your
Mind; Core Skills to Enhance your Performance, Well-being and
Integrity at work* Charlottesville VA: Hampton Roads, 2006

2. Morgan, Gareth: *Images of Organization* Thousand Oaks CA:
Sage Publications, 1997

3. Senge, Peter *The Fifth Discipline: The Art and Practice of the
Learning Organization* New York: Currency Doubleday, 1990

4. Seligman 2002; Haidt 2006.

5. Keyes, C.L.M. and Haidt, J. eds.. *Flourishing: Positive Psychology and the Life Well-Lived.* Washington, D.C.: American
Psychological Association, 2003

5. Sheldon, K. M., & Lyubomirsky, S. Achieving sustainable
new happiness: Prospects, practices, and prescriptions. In
A. Linley & S. Joseph Eds., *Positive psychology in practice* pp.
127-145. Hoboken, NJ: John Wiley & Sons 2004.

6. Kahneman D., & Riis J., Living, and Thinking About it:
Two Perspectives on Life. In F.A. Huppert, N. Baylis & B.
Keverne Eds. *The Science of Well-being,* Oxford: Oxford Uni-
versity Press, 2005

7. For simple techniques to achieve this see Hannam & Selby 2006

Conclusion: Spreading the Magic

1. For current statistics on the state of the world see: UN Human Development Report 2005
   http://hdr.undp.org/reports/global/2005/
   Worldwatch Institute Vital Signs
   http://www.worldwatch.org/node/4344
2. Max-Neff, M., Elizalde, A., and Hopenhayn, M. 1989 *'Human scale development: an option for the future'*, Development Dialogue, [1]: 5-81
3. For an overview of ecological footprints see
   http://www.footprintnetwork.org/gfn_sub.php?content=foot
   print_overview
   Work out your footprint at http://www.rprogress.org/
4. See City of Portland's website
   http://www.portlandonline.com/osd/
5. The quote is found on the website of the Memorial Museum of Space Exploration in Moscow:
   http://all-moscow.ru/culture/museum/astron/astro.en.html
6. Taken from the Slow Food website
   http://www.slowfood.com/about_us/eng/philosophy.lasso
7. See
   http://www.cittaslow.org.uk/page.php?Pid1=5&Pid2=11&P
   Lv=2
8. Elgin, Duane, *Voluntary Simplicity*. New York: William Morrow, 1998

And the website http://www.simpleliving.net/main/

9. Pernick, Ron & Wilder, Clint, *The Clean Tech Revolution* New York: HarperCollins, 2007.

10. ibid p19

11. See General Electric's website
    http://www.genewscenter.com/content/Detail.asp?ReleaseID=2333&NewsAreaID=2

12. www.terrain.org/articles/9/wann.htm
    http://www.newbelgium.com/sustainability.php

13. www.themagicofgroundhogday.com

14. The Earth Charter is an inspirational statement of values and vision for a sustainable planet, and I strongly recommend that you read it in detail http://www.earthcharter.org/

15. For a positive vision of individual and global change see Hartmann, T., *The Last Hours of Ancient Sunlight*, Three Rivers CA, 2004
    Korten, David C. *The Great Turning: From Empire to Earth Community*: San Francisco: Berrett-Koehler Publishers 2006
    Brown, Lester. *Plan B Rescuing a Planet under Stress and a Civilization in Trouble*, New York: Norton & Company, 2003

16. For an explanation of this idea see Metzner, Ralph, *Green Psychology, Transforming Our Relationship to Earth;* Rochester VT: Inner Traditions International, 1999

ABOUT THE AUTHOR

Entrepreneur

Paul is founder and Chairman of a successful computer recruitment and executive search business, which he set up in 1988. He has also set up training businesses, and co-founded his latest venture, Bright Green Talent, with the mission to recruit the brightest and the best talent in the world to work for organizations that are committed to sustainability and corporate social responsibility.

Teacher

Between 2001 and 2005 he was an Associate Fellow at the Oxford University Environmental Change Institute and was an Adjunct Fellow of Linacre College from 2002 to 2005.

Paul taught several modules on the Conservation and Nature, Society and Environmental Policy MSc programs. These include Organizational Behavior, and Environmental Leadership

Over the last 15 years he also trained thousands of people in the business and non-profit sector, including courses on Leadership, Sales, Change and Personal Development.

Consultant

Applying the same successful tools and practices from his own company he has provided consultant services to the following organizations: - Barclays Bank, British Airways, BT, BUPA, Canon, Express Newspapers, Fidelity Investments, Friends Provident, HSBC, Mars and many more.

His current consultancy focuses on Talent Management and Retention; Leadership; Motivation and Change Management.

Speaker

Paul has delivered many lectures to business, academic and non-profit audiences. He is available to give talks on a wide range of subjects including Talent, Leadership, Environmental Business and Change.

www.themagicofgroundhogday.com